TEACHING OF CIVICS AND POLITICAL SCIENCE

TEACHING OF CIVICS AND POLITICAL SCIENCE

Nirmal Yadav

ANMOL PUBLICATIONS PVT LTD
New Delhi-110 002

ANMOL PUBLICATIONS PVT LTD
4374 / 4B, Ansari Road
Daryaganj, New Delhi-110 002

Teaching of Civics and Political Science

First Edition 1994
ISBN 81-7041-963-8

Typesetted at
Chitra Computers
R/46, Rita Block, Shakarpur, Delhi-92

PRINTED IN INDIA

Published by J.L. Kumar for Anmol Publications Pvt. Ltd., New Delhi and Printed at Mehra Offset Press, Delhi.

Preface

This book primarily aims to serve a dual purpose. It is likely to serve the purpose of a text-book for prospective teachers, in India and some other South-East Asian Countries, who are looking forward for teaching of civics/political science in schools and colleges, secondly it is likely to serve as a reference book to the practising teachers. It is likely to help the students in understanding the aims, objectives, techniques and methods used for teaching of civics in schools. Each topic in the book has been divided into heads and sub-heads and the material has been presented in a proper sequence keeping in mind the examination requirements. The topics have been discussed in all their details and an attempt has been made to present the matter in a comprehensive and lucid manner.

It is hoped that the book will be appreciated by students and teachers alike. While preparing the book, material has been drawn from works of different authors, periodicals and journals and the author is indebted to all such persons and their publishers.

Author would also like to express his sincere gratitude to a number of friends and colleagues who have given many a valuable suggestions. Author is also thankful to his publishers.

Comments and suggestions for the improvement of the book will be gratefully accepted.

Author

Contents

Chapter 1

Meaning and Scope of Political Science/Civics

1.1 WHAT IS CIVICS ?

Civics is actually the social science, however in certain respects it forms a part of political science.

Civics is an old subject and previously it was taught alongwith history and political science. It was introduced as a separate subject only in the nineteenth century.

Origin of Civics

Man is a social animal and he is endowed with instinct of gregariousness. All his instincts are achieved and fulfilled in society. Man can make unhampered progress only in a well organised society. Society enables man to achieve talents and qualities by virtue of which he can make progress and achieve superiority over other living beings. Along-with his attempt to establish his superiority over other living beings man also makes efforts to resolve conflict and live in harmony with other social beings. He looks after the interests and requirements of his other fellow beings. **Civics** helps to resolve social conflicts in society and help man to live in harmony with his other fellow beings.

The word **Civics** is derived from the latin word '*Civis*' that means 'a citizen'. Another latin word '*Civitas*' means 'city state'. Both these words have given birth to the social science known as '**Civics**'.

In the ancient times, Rome and Greece, the two great states governed the various affairs with the help of the rules framed by the citizens of those states. They had their small city states known as 'civitas'. Afterwards the words 'civis' and 'civitas' came to English language and the words such as 'citizen' and 'city' etc., came into being.

In the modern times with the whole world becoming a single unit, the need for world fraternity has enormously increased and so the *civics* has assumed greater importance in the field of study.

Now we define *civics* as that branch of knowledge which deals with various aspects of social life of a citizen. Dr. E.M. White defines civics as under:

> "Civics is that more or less useful branch of human knowledge, which deals with every thing (social, intellectual, economical, political and even religious aspects) pertaining to citizenship, past, present and future, local, national, international and human."

In the words of Dr. Beni Prasad,

> "In the context of social relationship, there are many duties to be performed and correspondingly many sights to be respected. It is mainly with them that the civics is concerned."

This definition of civics lays more stress as the social life of the citizen.

In the words of F.J. Gould, "Civics is the study of institutions, habits and spirits by means of which a man or woman may fulfill the duties and receive the benefits of membership in political community."

In words of A.T. Shah, " Civics is that branch of human knowledge which deals with rights and duties of man living as a members of a group of people politically organized."

1.2 WHAT IS POLITICAL SCIENCE ?

Some definitions of political science are:

"Political Science begins and ends with the state."

J.W. Garner

"Political Science deals with the government."

S. Leacock

"Political Science deals with the general problems of the state and the government."

R.N. Gilchrist

"Political science is that part of the social science which deals with the foundations of the state and principles of government."

Javet Paul

Some writers like Bluntschli, Gavies and Garner are of the view that political science in the study of state alone and they exclude the study of government from the scope of political science.

In words of Catlin, "Political science is the study of acts of human and social control or the study of control, relationship of wills."

Raymond Aron writes that in France there is no political science in the singular. The term used is political and moral (or political, economic and social) sciences.

1.3 IS CIVICS A SCIENCE OR AN ART ?

Some thinker consider civics as a science (i.e. a social science).

Social sciences are different from physical sciences (e.g. physics, chemistry, biology etc.). Social sciences follow the methodology of sciences in observation, collection of data, its classification and laying down of theories etc., but these theories are not very mathematical and rigid. Theories change with change in socio-economic conditions. Social sciences have there own rules. Civics is thus a science but not at all a physical science.

Lord Bryce views civics to be as good a science as Astronomy. It simply implies that in civics we cannot have only conjectures and we have to base our knowledge on solid foundations. Thus from the point of view of science, civics is a systematised body of knowledge that deals with citizenship.

Some other writers consider civics as an art only. Truely speaking **art** is nothing but the practical application of the knowledge acquired by the science. Keeping this in view we find that civics is both an art and a science. Civics not only collects knowledge in a systematic manner, about citizenship, and also puts it into practice.

In the words of Dr. Beni Prasad, "civics is both science and art in the sense that it investigates conditions and seeks to apply the results of its investigations to the furtherance of human welfare."

1.4 VARIOUS DIVISIONS OF POLITICAL SCIENCE

The International Political Science Association formed in 1948 under the auspices of UNESCO, suggested that the subject should be divided into the following four fields with their sub-divisions:

(a) Political Theory

(i) Political theory

(ii) History of Political ideas.

(b) Political Institutions

(i) The Constitution

(ii) National Government

(iii) Regional and Local Government

(iv) Public Administration

(v) Economic and Social Functions of Government

(vi) Comparative Political Institutions.

(c) Parties, Groups and Public Opinion

(i) Political Parties

(ii) Groups and Associations

(iii) Participation of the citizens in the Government and the Administration.

(iv) Public opinion.

(d) International Relations

(i) International Politics

(ii) International Organisation and Administration

(iii) International Law.

1.5 SCOPE OF POLITICAL SCIENCE

The subject which deals with man in relation to the state and government is known as *political science*. Political science is a branch of study which is concerned with the political aspects of man's life in society as distinct from the economic, philosophical, ethical and other aspects.

Dorothy Pickles has explained the meaning, significance and scope of political science as, "when men begin to speculate about the rules by which they are governed ... when they begin to ask whether these rules aught to be accepted ... why some societies chose different rules from others, whether it is possible to find the best rules for a particular society, or whether it is possible to diverse general rules of conduct which could or should be applicable to all societies. In order to answer these questions, they are obliged to make more fundamental inquiries into the purposes for which human societies exist, and their relations to their purposes of human life itself."

The nature, content and scope of political science have changed from time to time. In more recent years the centre of interest has been particularly to the relation and pattern of interaction among individuals.

A new thought that has recently emerged in France suggests that the division of social sciences into separate branches, as political sciences, sociology, economics, ethics etc., is not a logical analysis of the affairs relating to the organised society. They all constitute one integrated study of man and society and one cannot be separated from the other as all act and react upon one another. They should, therefore, come under the same umbrella and be named as political sciences.

We can summarise the scope of political science as under:

(i) It deals with the study of man as an individual as well as in totality of his social relations.

(ii) It is a dimension of social process.

(iii) It serves the general interest of the society.

(iv) It is a process to bring about changes in society. It is only a means and not an end.

(v) It is a scientific study of society and classes rather than individuals or groups.

(vi) It cannot be studied and understood scientifically without associating it with economic, legal, social, moral, cultural and ideological structures.

(vii) It is needed for resolving the conflict of various interests, maintain unity, cooperation and order in society.

1.6 IMPORTANCE OF CIVICS/POLITICAL SCIENCE AND ITS PLACE IN CURRICULUM

Any society takes care of its young through the home and the school. It is through its schools, that a society prepares its future citizens. In a developing society like ours this responsibility of the school in greater, because the school should not only transmit, from one generation to the next, our tradition and culture, but help in the process of modernisation. For discharging this responsibility, the school depends, among other things, heavily on the teaching of civics, the central concern of which is to understand the relationship between man and his society.

A study of civics helps us to develop a broad, rational, national and secular outlook. The Secondary Education Commission 1952-53 has observed, "The education system must make its contribution to the development of habits, attitudes and qualities of character, which will enable its citizens to bear worthily the responsibilities of democratic citizenships and to counteract all those fissiparous tendencies which hinder the emergence of a broad national and secular outlook."

Place of Civics in Curriculum

In this respect there is a good deal of controversy. Some scholars are of the opinion that it is a very important social science and so it must find a place in curriculum while others disagree with it. Those who disagree argue that the subject matter of civics is found in other social sciences and so it is of no use to teach civics as a separate subject.

The modern educational theory feels that civics must find a place in the curriculum, because it teaches us the various rules and regulations of ideal citizenship and it also encourages people to put these rules into practice. Some of the arguments that are forwarded for inclusion of civics in the curriculum are as under:

1. Those who are students today will become the citizens tomorrow and so they should know their rights and duties as good citizens. They can be taught about these by civics.
2. In any democracy political consciousness is of fundamental

importance and it is essential to have political and social consciousness in young men. It can be achieved by the study of civics.

3. For real progress of society co-operation and co-existence are essential. These virtues and values can be taught by the teaching of civics.
4. To lead a successful life one must be familiar with the obligations of a social being. The study of civics can impart such a knowledge to our youth.
5. The study of civics is also essential to learn the art of becoming an able administrator.
6. Study of civics helps to develop in the child a national and an international outlook. Such an outlook is essential in this age of internationalism.
7. Study of civics also help children to acquire a scientific outlook which is very necessary to our students.

Importance of Teaching of Civics in India and its Place in the National Education System

Civics as a subject occupies an important place in Indian national educational system. Through civics teaching we can create a broad, national and secular outlook in our children. In this respect we quote here from the report of the Secondary Education Commission presided over by Dr. Mudaliar—

> "The education system must make its contribution to the development of habits, attitudes and qualities of character which will enable its citizens to bear worthily the responsibilities of democratic citizenship and to counteract all those fissaparous tendencies which hinder the emergence of a broad national and secular outlook."

Since civics teaches us about citizenship so it occupies an important place in our educational system. The study of civics is quite helpful to become an ideal citizen. Patric Geddes has remarked that, "Civics is the youngest and last branch of science as yet, a little noticed on the vast and ever spreading tree of knowledge which may be recognised as one of the most fruitful of all."

Following limes clearly bring about the importance of teaching of civics for success of democracy. "In a democracy, if it is anything more than the thoughtless exercise of vote, an individual must form his own independent judgement on all kinds of complicated, social, economic and political issues and, to a large extent, decide his own course of action."

This can be achieved to a great extent by the teaching of civics.

Teaching of civics is also quite helpful in eradication of a number of social evils prevalent in our country.

1.7 CONCEPT OF POLITICAL SCIENCE IN ANCIENT INDIA

The Arthasastra of Kautilya

Arthasastra is unique in ancient classics on the science of polity. Kautilya's Arthasastra superseded all his predecessors. Kautilya proclaimed that politics was a supreme science and an art. *Arthasastra* contains 15 books or parts. It deals exhaustively with various problems connected with kingship, civil administration, criminal and personal law, duties and responsibilities of courtiers and retainers of the king. It also describe the nature and functions of the seven *prakiritis* (elements) of the state. The seven elements of state according to Kautilya are:

(i) *Swami* (the king) (ii) *Amatya* (ministers) (iii) *Jampads* (people and territory) (iv) *Durg* (Fort) (v) *Kosha* (Treasury) (vi) *Dands* (Force) and (vii) *Mitra* (Allies or Friends).

Kautilya has dealt with the minutest details of state craft.

Gandhian Political Thought

Gandhi's Political thought is based on religion and morality. Actually Gandhian political thought is a way of life. Gandhi wanted to purify the political life, to kindle love in human mind, to rehabilitate the freedom of man and to restore and teach the dignity of human labour. Gandhiji considered 'Satyagraha' and 'non-violence' as the supreme concepts to reform politics and all his politics was based on religion. It can be easily said that Gandhiji worked for the spiritualisation of politics. Gandhiji being a believer of trusteeship visualised an enlightened society where in social life was based not on external free but on internal control. In such a society every one rules over himself and regulates his own actions in the interests of the society. Everything in such a society is based on voluntary organisation. The ideal society will be like a family. Failing such an ideal society, Gandhiji preferred a non-violent state with limited functions and social welfare as its end.

Revision Questions

1. What is civics ? Is it a science or an art ?
2. Discuss the importance of civics in the Indian national education system.
3. What is the scope of teaching of civics ?

Chapter 2

Aims and Objectives of Teaching of Civics

2.1 INTRODUCTION

For proper teaching of a subject it is essential to have a knowledge of aims and objectives of the subject. This is also true for the teaching of civics. Various methods of teaching are then evolved according to these aims and objectives. For determining the aims of teaching any subject we have to take into into consideration the utility and usefulness of that subject. We have material as well as spiritual aspects in our life. For a successful spiritual life it is essential that we have a well founded material life.

The aims and objectives of teaching various subjects are normally very similar and they are generally guided by economic and social considerations. The aims and objectives of teaching civics include all the aims and objectives of education. Different writers have listed these aims and objectives in different ways. In case of civics, it is said that, "The outstanding purpose of instructions in civics is to produce citizens and to aid pupils in the formation of a higher type of civic character."

2.2 AIMS OF TEACHING OF CIVICS

Aims are broad general statements that communicate long range purposes or intentions. A very general aim can be broken down into different kinds of objectives. Objectives are more precise statements of purpose. The aims and objectives cannot remain the same in all times and under all circumstances. The teacher should utilize these aims and objectives in such a way that he may produce ideal citizens of the country. Some important aims of teaching civics are given below:

1. Ideal Citizenship

The most important aim of teaching civics is to produce ideal citizens i.e., to imbibe in students all the qualities of an ideal citizen.

Characteristics of a Good Citizen

A good citizen

(i) Believes in equality of opportunity for all people.

(ii) Values, respects and defends basic human rights and privileges guaranteed by our constitution.

(iii) Respects and upholds the low and its various agencies.

(iv) Understands and accepts the democratic principles.

(v) Puts the general welfare above his own welfare.

(vi) Exercises his right of vote freely.

(vii) Accepts his civic responsibility and discharges them to the best of his capability.

(viii) Realises the necessary connection of education with democracy.

(ix) Assumes a personal responsibility for the wise use of natural resources.

(x) Understands cultures and ways of life other than his own.

(xi) Supports all efforts to prevent war, but is always ready to depend his country against tyranny and aggression.

(xii) Cultivates qualities of character and personality that have a high value in his culture.

(xiii) Recognises taxes as payment for community services and pays them promptly.

(xiv) In a responsible family member and assumes his full responsibility for maintaining the civic standards of his neighbourhood and community.

(xv) In guided by the idea of "Live and Let Live."

Writing about citizenship H.H. Horne observes, "Citizenship is a man's place in the States. As the State in one of the permanent institutions of society and as man must ever live in organised relation with his follows citizenship cannot be omitted from the constituency of the educational ideal."

Even Greek philosophers have recognised that ideal citizenship is the main aim of the Civics. This is contained in the 'Civic Oath':

> "We will never bring disgrace to this our city by any act of dishonesty or cowardice, nor desert our suffering comrades. We will fight for the ideals and sacred things of the city, alone and with many; we will reverse and obey the city's laws and do our best to incite alike respect in those among us who are prone to annul them or set them at naught; we will strive unceasingly to quicken the public sense of civic thought. Thus in all these ways we will transmit this city and not only not less, but greater, better, more beautiful than it was transmitted to us."

The Secondary Education Commission appointed by the Government of India also recognised this fact and gave it out in its report, as shall be evident from the following lines:

> "To be effective, a democratic citizen should have the understanding and the intellectual integrity to sift truth from falsehood, facts from propaganda, to reject the dangerous appeal of fanaticism and prejudice. He must develop a scientific attitude of mind of think objectively and base his conclusions on tested data. He should have an open mind receptive to new ideas and not confined within one prison walls of out-moded customs, traditions and beliefs. It should neither reject the old because it is old nor accept the new because it is new, but dispassionately examine both and courageously reject whatever arrests the forces of justice and progress."

Report of the Secondary Education Commission (Government of India).

2. National Character and Patriotism

No country can progress effectively unless its citizens are soaked in the spirit of patriotism. They should be prepared to sacrifice everything for their motherland. They should also be proud of their cultural heritage and uphold the values of the society. These things can be inculcated only if the teacher of Civics tries to handle them at their impressionable age, in a psychological and scientific manner. He should try to develop national character in them and base it on the virtues of co-operation, love, sympathy etc.

3. Development of Democratic Outlook and Strengthening Democracy

Teaching of civics should aim at giving practical training of citizenship to the students. It should inculcate in the young souls the democratic outlook. For our young democracy a study of civics can help a lot to develop proper attitudes in young pupils, which can ultimately strengthen our democracy.

4. Political Consciousness and Social Efficiency

Teaching of civics should aim at generating political consciousness in the students. It should make them socially efficient. They should be well-aware of the social and political problems of the country and should try to take active part in them. It is the students of today on whom depends the future of the country. Social efficiency requires the young students to have the qualities of sympathy, co-operation, patriolism etc. Such qualities can be developed in pupils only by teaching of civics in a scientific manner.

5. Scientific Outlook

In this age of science, each one of us must posses a scientific outlook i.e., to look at things in their proper perspective. This should be one of the main aims of teaching civics. It would help the young ones to leave unscientific and unnecessary things in their life.

6. Strengthening National and International Integration

In a vast country like India, a member of fissiparous tendencies are likely to exist and such tendencies may threaten the unity of county. This is a serious problem. A proper teaching of civics can help to create a sound base for the continued oneness and unity of country.

With the development of science and technology, the barriers of time and space are crumbling down. It is not far off, when the whole world will become a single unit. Any citizen of a country will then not be able to keep himself away from the ways of other countries. A man can be a real citizen of his country only when he possesses an international outlook. Such an outlook will help him to acquire the attitude of 'Co-existence' or the principle of 'Live and Let Live'.

7. Promoting Rational Outlook

Various evils, exist even today, which eat into the vitals of the society (e.g. untouchability regionalism, casteism etc.). By proper teaching of civic it is possible to make a sound base against these social evils in the minds of the pupil in their going age.

8. Strengthening Common Ideas of Various Faiths

There are many common ideas in various faiths. Almost all faiths such as Buddhism, *Christianity, Confusciasm. Judaism, Hinduism, Islam* etc., believe in peace and brotherhood, non-violence and coexistence, truth etc. such common ideas can be strengthened by teaching of civics.

2.3 OBJECTIVES OF TEACHING OF CIVICS

The objectives are the specific and precise behavioural outcome of teaching a particular topic in civics. For example, the goal 'promotion of International understanding' might include the following objectives:

(i) Learning and recalling knowledge about other countries.

(ii) Inquiring into problems relating to other countries.

(iii) Appreciating cultural aspects of other countries.

(iv) Developing skills in relating to people of other countries.

Here we discuss some important objectives of teaching of civics. It is hoped that such a discussion will assist teacher in teaching and also in evaluating his work in classroom.

Bloom's Taxonomy of Objectives

Bloom's taxonomy of objectives is a classification of instructional objectives in a hierarchy. According to it specific objectives have been classified into the following three categories:

(i) Cognitive domain objectives.

(ii) Affective domain objectives.

(iii) Psychomotor domain objectives.

The cognitive domain objectives include knowledge, understandings, applications, analysis, synthesis and evaluation.

The effective domain objectives include the appreciations, values, attitudes, interests and feelings.

The psychomotor domain objectives include skills.

Some of these are discussed here.

(i) Intellectual Development. The basic objective of education is to bring about an all round development of the personality of the child. All round development includes the intellectual development. A proper intellectual development is a must for any proper cultural consciousness. To earn a livelihood is not the sole objective of life. One needs leisure after earning his livelihood and one should be able to spend one's leisure time properly and usefully.

This leisure time should be used for intellectual and spiritual development for a balanced growth of human race. It is only through the intellectual development that we can distinguish between good and bad. This power of distinguishing between good and bad is essential to become a successful member of society.

(ii) Knowledge of the World and the Broadening Outlook. Civics teaching provides to the pupil a knowledge of the different people of the world and contributions made by them for the development of world culture. Such a knowledge broadens our outlook and bring about the development of world brotherhood and world citizenship.

Through the knowledge of civics the pupil realises the interdependence of mankind. He also becomes familiar with the differences in the physical character of the people and understands the such differences are due to variations in physical environments. Thus we find that development of the international outlook is one of the aims and objectives of teaching of civics.

(iii) Understanding. Teaching of Civics should enable the pupils to understand that:

1. The basic requirements such as food, cloths and shelter of man all over the world are the same and man always seeks the help of others in meeting these needs.

2. Man's life on earth is closely connected with his physical environment. His activities are governed by it, though he has always been striving, with varying success to turn it to his advantage also.

3. Man's life has become possible by the use of physical resources, such as soil, water, forests, minerals. Man requires these resources, badly and it is his duty, therefore, to conserve them and to put them to the best possible use.

4. Man lives in society. He has to depend on others for his requirements. Thus members of a family, states of the country and different countries of the world are dependent one on another. Life is impossible without co-operation.

5. Mutual co-operation, good will, trust and a sense of responsibility are an essential pre-requisite for smooth and peaceful life in the society.

6. In the democratic, socialist, secular republic of India all citizens have equal rights and duties. Students should understand these fully and discharge them conscientiously.

7. There is a great diversity among the people in the different parts of our country with respect to languages, food habits, dresses and religious beliefs. In spite of all these differences we all are Indians and make one nation.

8. India has her own culture and Indians cherish certain values. To preserve and modify our culture and values it is essential to know these.

9. Many a great men have contributed to the development of Indian culture. We should know something about these greatmen.

10. No doubt there is a great diversity in different countries but all countries are a part of one world. Each country has some important contribution. We should show the same respect to the people of each country and should honour the differences in their religious beliefs and faiths.

(iv) Skills and Abilities. 1. While taking part of meetings and working in groups children should be able:

— to express themselves clearly and logically through speech or writing.

— to listen to others with due respect and attention.

— to use respectful language during conversation and to speak on one's turn.

— to discharge assigned responsibilities, to co-operate with others and to be able to lead others.

— to take active part in meetings, debates, dramas and other activities and to work systematically.

— to arrange exhibitions.

— to collect information from different sources, to present it, to use it and to write brief reports.

2. While visiting important places of neighbourhood, children should be able:

— to plan tours and excursions.

— to be courteous and respectful towards others.

— to co-operate and to share things with others.

— to understand the traffic signs and follow the traffic rules.

3. While using maps, charts, graphs and globes children should be able:

— to identify, read and compare different types of maps.

— to measure the distance between two places on the map.

— to locate different places on the map.

— to read directions on the map.

— to know and understand the meaning of colours and symbols used in maps.

— to understand the difference between a globe and a map.

— to read easy and simple charts and graphs.

—to prepare simple charts and models.

—to arrange in the album pictures, flowers, leaves and newspaper clippings.

(v) Attitudes. The teaching of civics should develop in the pupil the following attitudes:

1. Respect for people of different religions, communities, languages and occupations.
2. Respect for and pride in the national goals and values.
3. Faith in country's unity.
4. Respect for national symbols.
5. Accepting small responsibilities for the sake of the country.
6. Keen desire to preserve country's independence.
7. Willingness to share responsibility to preserve personal or government property and the natural resources of the country.
8. Respect for law and government.
9. Respect for teachers and elders.
10. Sympathy for the poor and the helpless.
11. Faith in international understanding and co-operation.
12. Appreciation of natural beauty.
13. Awareness towards change.
14. Self-reliance.

(Adopted from *Social Studies Teaching Manual*, NCERT, New Delhi).

Objectives of Teaching Civics for Classes III to V

NCERT syllabi for Classes III to V in accordance with the nationally developed curriculum for the ten-year school states:

For Classes III, IV and V, a course in Environmental Studies I (social studies) would be introduced. This course at this stage consists of a broad and composite instructional area which draws its information from different social sciences such as history, geography, civics and economics in order to develop social values and attitudes which are in conformity with the cultural heritage of our society and its accepted goals. The general objectives for teaching this course at the primary school stage are as follows:

1. To help the child to explore and understand his social and cultural environment.
2. To develop in the child a sense of belongingness to the society through a gradual widening of mental horizons—from his home and school to the wider world.
3. To acquaint the child with the world of work and to develop in him respect for human labour.
4. To encourage the child to understand that we are striving to build a better life for all.
5. To impress on the child's mind, as he grows, that ours is a rich and composite culture in the formation of which people of different faiths, regions, and linguistic groups, have made valuable contributions.
6. To develop among children respect for all religions and their places and ways of worships.
7. To encourage the child to understand that we are all equal irrespective of sex, creed, language, etc., and that there are no superior or inferior people and that we all co-operate and organise ourselves to solve our problems; and
8. To impress on the child that India, in keeping with its cultural heritage, is one of the important countries of the world that is active in promoting peace, understanding and co-operation among the nations of world.

Objectives of Civics in Classes VI to VIII

Civics as a constituent of Social Sciences. NCERT Syllabi for Classes VI to VIII in accordance with the nationally developed curriculum for the ten-year school gives the following objectives:

The course in civics has the major responsibility of promoting well-informed and intelligent citizens who have the ability to participate in the affairs of their community effectively. From this point of view, the course at this stage aims mainly at imparting training in civic life rather than mere scholarship. It contains such socially imperative knowledge which would also provide training in the development of civic competencies. Some practical aspects of citizenship education have also been incorporated from the point of view of adopting a functional approach. Thus the syllabus in civics at the middle stage has the following objectives:

1. To provide the student with intelligent understanding of the various social responsibilities and civic processes.
2. To help the student understand our constitution and the values enshrined in it.
3. To acquaint the student with the machinery of the government at different levels.
4. To make the student conscious of the actual problems that are facing our country today and install in him a sense of responsibility towards the community.
5. To make the student identify with the people and their institutions.
6. To inculcate in the student the values of democracy, secularism, socialism and national integration.

Project Work

The student who is a citizen in training, needs help in getting experience and insight into the process of citizenship. Under this scheme an opportunity should be provided to the student to develop abilities which are essential for any active citizen in India.

It is suggested that 20 per cent of the total marks allotted to civics should be assigned to the project work. Every student should take up at least two practical activities every year and prepare a short write-up or report on his project. The reports of the students should be evaluated on the basis of three components:

1. Collection of data;
2. Analysis and interpretation of data; and
3. Conclusions drawn on the basis of this interpretation.

List of Projects

Note: This is not an exhaustive list. Other projects of such type could also be taken up.

(i) Sanitation problem of any town of the area.

(ii) Management and maintenance of civic amenities in the area and the related problems.

(iii) Functioning of police in the area.

(iv) Distribution and location of educational institutions in the area—nursery, primary, middle, secondary, technical, aided and unaided, for boys and girls, etc.

(v) Organising school, government and national festivals.

(vi) Election process from nomination to declaration of results of elections of students' union, village panchayats, municipal committees.

(vii) Study of some major developments in the national life, e.g., electrification, nationalisation of banks, nuclear experiment, food, population, green revolution, white revolution, impact of 20-point programme in the locality, study of local historical events connected with the Indian Independence Movement.

(viii) Participation of local people in war effort during Indo-Pak and Sino-Indian Wars.

(ix) Achievements and problems of any one of the following:

(a) Village Panchayat/Municipal Committee or Corporation.

(b) Block Samiti.

(c) Zila Parishad.

Objectives of Civics in Classes IX and X

The curriculum for the ten-year school—A framework of NCERT states the objectives of Civics as under:

The major objective of the study of the social sciences is to acquaint the child with his past and present geographical and social environment. An effective programme of teaching of the social sciences in schools should help the pupils to take a keen interest in the ways people live and function through various socio-economic and political institutions. It should also help children to develop an insight into human relationship, social values and attitudes. These are essential to enable the growing citizen of tomorrow to participate effectively in the affairs of the community, the state, the country, and the world at large.

The teaching of the social sciences should enable children to appreciate India's rich cultural heritage as also to recognize and get rid of what is undesirable and antiquated, especially in the context of the social change. The schools should see that narrow parochial, chauvinistic and obscurantist tendencies are not allowed to grow in our pupils. The schools should endeavour to develop a will and ability in every pupil to participate in the most important task of the reconstruction of our society and economy with a sense of social commitment. Children should also develop a faith in the destiny of our nation in terms of promoting a spirit of tolerance and assimilation, the peace and harmony among the peoples of the world. Thus instruction in the social science should promote the values and ideals of humanism, secularism, socialism and democracy. It should inculcate attitudes and impart the knowledge, necessary for the achievement of the principal values of just world order, maximisation of economic and social welfare, minimisation of violence and maximisation of ecological stability.

The study of the social sciences in Classes I-X should include the study of history, geography, civics and economics. In view of the limited time that will be available for each of these branches, it would be desirable to integrate there teaching in a way that the pupils develop a proper understanding of the facts and problems in the right perspective without causing any damage to the totality of the individual disciplines. This would require identifying the essential units in each of the subjects and then into an integrated syllabus for the social sciences.

Since Classes V, VIII, and X are the terminal classes for a large number of students, it is necessary to develop self-contained courses of study for each stage, and at the same time the course should be such as to lay foundations for the subsequent stage. While following this principle, it is also necessary to avoid repetition and waste of time and every as far as possible.

Revision Questions

1. Bring out clearly the importance of teaching civics is schools.
2. What are the aims of teaching civics ?
3. What are the objectives of teaching civics ?
4. What are the aims and objectives of teaching civics as a subject at the secondary stage ?

Chapter 3

Correlation of Civics with Other Subjects

3.1 INTRODUCTION

The major aims of education is the unification of knowledge existing in different branches of learning. To achieve such a unification a conscious effort has to be made by teachers teaching various subjects. It is only in such joint ventures that we will be able to achieve the goal of unification of knowledge and bridge the gap that separates them

3.2 IMPORTANCE OF CORRELATION

This is the age of correlationship and no subjects can be taught in isolation. It is only for convenience of study that we have splitted the knowledge into different subjects but no subject is completely aloof from others and it has to be correlated with other subjects.

Modern educationists have no doubt in their mind about the fact that the *teaching of a particular subject should be carried out in correlation with other subjects.* The correlation is more between those subjects that have a common bearing. There are various types of correlationships and every type of correlationship has its importance in the education in different ways. The two important types of correlation are:

(i) Correlation with daily life.

(ii) Correlation with other subjects.

It was Herbert who first conceived the idea of correlating the teaching of various subjects. Later a Zillar made this theory of correlation more elaborate. Then De Garmo and John Devey put more stress on the integration in teaching of various subjects. Today it is considered essential to correlate the teaching of civics. T. Raymond has remarked—

"No subject in ever well-understand and no art is intelligently practiced, if the light which the other studies are able to throw upon it is deliberately shut out."

3.3 KINDS OF CORRELATION

Correlation and co-ordination may be of the following types:

(i) Vertical correlation

(ii) Horizontal Correlation

(iii) Correlation with practical life.

(i) Vertical Correlation

In this type of correlation an attempt is made to correlate the teaching of various divisions of a subject. An attempt is also made to make the subject taught in lower classes useful for the teaching of the same subject in the higher classes.

(ii) Horizontal Correlation

In this type of correlation an attempt is made to co-ordinate the teaching of various subjects. It can be achieved by any of the two methods (i.e. casual or systematic).

(iii) Correlation with Practical Life

According to Herbert Spenser the main aim of education is to prepare the students for future life. To achieve this aim education is correlated with life. Thus the teaching of various subjects should be correlated with various aspects of life.

3.4 CORRELATION OF CIVICS WITH OTHER SUBJECTS

All the social sciences deal with the study of various aspects of human life and its various activities. In political science we are mainly concerned with the study of man's political behaviour in association with other men as member of a common society. Thus there is more correlation between political science and other social sciences. This fact has been closely brought about by Janet Paul in his observation, "Political science is closely connected with political economy or the science of wealth, with law either natural or positive, which occupies itself principally with the relations of citizens one to another, with history which furnishes the facts of which it has need, with philosophy, and especially with morals, which give to it a part of its principles."

While studying the correlation between political science (civics) with other subjects, following points may be kept in view:

1. Political science is indebted to other social sciences upto a certain extent.
2. Other social sciences take help from political science.
3. These subjects, though, are interdependent yet they enjoy an independent status.

Civics is a social science and its correlation is more other branches of social science.

Civics and Sociology

Sociology deals with the study of various social relations of man. In this we mainly deal with the development of human as a social being. In it we also study the economic, religious, moral and political developments of society. It thus is quite natural for civics to form a part of the study of sociology.

We find that sociology deals with all the aspects of man's life and here we mention that civics deals only with the civic aspect of the social life of man. Civics teaches them (human beings) about their rights and duties as good citizens. It also tells them about the ways and means through which political and social developments, maybe made. It may be said that civics deals man only as a citizen while sociology studies man as a social being.

Teaching of sociology and civics is therefore correlated and this correlationship is quite natural and beneficial.

Writing about the relation of political science and sociology Garner has observed, "The state is a sociological as well as a political phenomenon and during its early stages it was in fact more of a social than a political institution." Similarly Franklin H. Giddings has stated, " To teach the theory of the state to men who have not learnt the first principle of sociology, is like teaching astronomy or thermodynamics to men who have not learnt the Newtonian Law of Motion."

2. Civics and Psychology

According to Professor Garner, "Government to be stable and really popular must reflect and express the mental ideas and moral sentiments of those who are subject to its authority. In short it must be in harmony with 'mental consultation' of the race." In the general elections political leaders make all possible efforts to play with the sentiments of the people. Graham Wallas and W.H.R. Rivers in their books, *Human Nature in politics* and *Psychology* and *politics* emphasised the relationship of politics and psychology.

"Civics is a science which studies the condition of the best possible social life."

It is only one aspect of human life. It is most necessary to develop only one aspect of the life of an individual. An attemt should be made to develop the various aspects of human life. Different subjects deal with different aspects of human life. An attempt be made to correlate the study of all such subjects. Making his observations about this Prof. White has remarked—

> "Civics is essentially a subject of connections, it links all times and periods as parts of a long chain of achievements beaten out of civilisations, it connects, all subjects as parts of the life of the story of mankind."

From this observation it becomes evident that civics does not confine itself to the teaching of citizenship only. It attempts to deal with various aspects of human life.

3. Civics and History

John Seelay has observed "History without political science has no fruit, political science without history has no root." The inter-dependence of two subjects is so great that they touch each other frequently.

Burgess states, " Separate them (History and political science) and one becomes cripple, if not a corpse and other a will of the wisp."

Professor Garner states, " To fully comprehend political science in its fundamental relations we must study it historically and to interpret history in its true significance we must study them politically."

History is the systematic study of the past events that have taken place in society, social, political, economic, moral etc. The subject matter of civics is not one sided. Civics only deals, with the civic life of an individual while History deals with all the aspects of human life in the past. Lord Sextor has rightly remarked—

> "The science of politics is the science that picks up the grains of gold from the sand of the river bed of history and forms a presentable ornament."

Civics is concerned with various social and political problems because they affect the civic life of an individual. History deals with the study of the past whereas Civics is the study of he contemporary facts. To study the past we shall have to delve deep while for the study of the civic problems no such efforts are required.

The subject matter of History has a strong bearing on Civics. We cannot make progress in the present unless we have an idea of the past Civics draws on the funds of History to get knowledge of the past attempts of people in solving the different civic problems.

For a very long time History and Civics were studied together. It is through the example of History that the teacher of Civics can inculcate the qualities of discipline, patriotism, social services, etc., in the students. It is these qualities that make a man ideal citizen. In order to become an ideal citizen one has to take advantage of the stock of History. Prof. Jones has rightly remarked—

> "History is veritable mind of life experiences and the youth of today studies History that he may provide by the experiences of the race."

With the knowledge of History, a student of Civics can know the attitude of the rulers in the past towards citizens. He can also know about the results of the attitude of the rulers. In the light of the knowledge acquired, the student of Civics can utilise the present day situations and bring about a good social and civic order.

Patriotism is an integral part of good citizenship. This quality can be develop in the students through the examples of great men of history e.g. Shivaji, Maharana Pratap etc. By the example of Akbar the quality of secularism can be developed. By quoting Mahatma Gandhi we can develop in students the habit of non-violence and inspire the students to make sacrifices.

It becomes quite clear that the knowledge of history in useful in teaching of Civics and so a horizontal correlationship be developed between teaching of history and Civics Prof. Sealey has rightly remarked,

"History without civics has no root and civics without history bears no fruit."

4. Civics and Economics

Economics is a social science. In the past economics was known as 'political economy'. In economics we deal with production, distribution and exchange of the wealth.

In modern times MacIver and Marx have considered both economics and political science to be closely related. Economic situations have a decisive say in the political life of a country.

The knowledge of economics helps the civics to a great extent. Economics inspires human beings to perform certain acts of human welfare. A knowledge of civics is quite useful in dealing with laboures and consumers in a reasonable and judicious manner. If economic relations are not properly established it becomes very different to establish proper social and civic relations. Thus, we find that economic development forms the basis of various developments—social, cultural, moral, religious, aesthetic etc.

About a correlation between economics and civics it has been rightly said, "Economics as an art depends on civics and civics as an art depends on economics. They are supplementary an complementary to each other."

5. Civics and Geography

In the study of political science the most important thing is the study of administration of particular unit and the problems associated with it. There are wide differences in administration in different lands. These differences may be attributed to difference in geographical conditions. In some countries we find that democracy has survived very long years which has been possible only because of geographical factors (e.g., as in Switzerland).

Geography studies the natural problems of the world. It is, therefore, natural for it to be correlated with Civics.

With the help of the knowledge of geography we can have an idea about the culture and the way of living of the people of a country. Civics can take advantage of this knowledge.

To understand the different political set ups in different countries we have to understand the differences in geographical factors in those countries. The role America and Russia and their present position is world polity is also due to certain geographical factors. The main point of contention between world powers has been there anxiety to have control over oil rich South-East Asian region.

Although teaching of Civics and Geography is done independently of each other but they are corelated. They form part of the group of the social sciences called social studies. Both these sciences aim at human welfare. One presents the background while the other can play on that background. The teacher of Civics should make an effort to correlate the geographical factors with the teaching of the Civics. He can very safely lay down rules and ways of making civic life happy, taking advantage of the knowledge of the geographical factors. In short, both these things are correlated.

6. Civics and General Science

General Science deals with the principles of the science. Actually it has very little to do with Civics. Under General Science we have the knowledge of the various factors of human life. Hygiene sometimes forms a part of General Science, so we can say that Civics in indirectly related to General Science. Directly speaking the teaching of the two cannot be correlated.

7. Correlationship between the Teaching of Civics and the Literature

Literature reflects different social, economic, religious, political and moral problems of the society. Some one has said that literature is the mirror of the society. The writer view the society from its own angle and tries to present it before the readers. Through this knowledge the society can be improved.

Civic aims at development ideal citizenship. This is based on certain ideals and values. The writer can inculcate these ideals and values in the young ones, without making them feel that certain things are being taught to them. Mahatma Gandhi presented the ideals of truth and non-violence. A literature can inculcate these ideals in the young students indirectly.

Thus, we can say that the writer tries to teach the principle of Civics to the young students, in an indirect manner.

Correlation between the teaching of various subjects is quite helpful for the development of the personality of the students. Various ideals of social life are reflected in different social sciences. If the teaching is conducted in a co-ordinated and correlated manner, the development of the personality is likely to be balanced and scientific.

8. Political Science and Ethics

The close correlation between political science and ethics is reflected in Plato's observation, "Good citizens can be formed in a good state." Hegel considers the state to be the highest expression of morality. In the words of Mahatma Gandhi, "What is morally wrong, cannot be politically right". Chankya considers that *politics without religion is monstrous.* Ivor Brown writes, " Politics is nothing but ethics at large..... Ethical theory is incomplete without political theory, become man is an associated creature and cannot live fully in isolation. Political theory is idle without ethical theory because its study and its results depend fundamentally upon our scheme of moral values, our conceptions of right and wrong."

9. Political Science and Public Administration

According to D. White the scope and purpose of public administration, "The immediate objective of the art of public administration is the most efficient utilisation of resources at the disposal of officials and employees."

In their broader context the ends of administration are the ultimate objectives of the state—the maintainance of peace and order, the progressive achievements of justice, etc. This points to a very close relationship between political science and public administration. Thus we find a close correlation between political science and public administrations.

Revision Questions

1. How will you correlate the teaching of civics with other school subjects ?

2. Discuss the various ways of correlating the teaching of civics with other branches of social studies.

3. Discuss the correlation of civics with history, Geography and Economics.

4. Is there any correlation between civics and general science ? If yes, illustrate.

Chapter 4

Curriculum of Civics/Political Science

4.1 INTRODUCTION

'Curriculum' may be defined as the 'social environment is motion'. It is the sum total of all the activities and experiences provided by the school to the learners for achieving the desired objectives. The courses of studies are merely a suggestion for curriculum activities and procedures, a guide for teaching to follow.

Curriculum is the pivot and hub around which all activities in school revolve. Curriculum in political science/civics is the part of the school curriculum which includes the subject matter and experiences that is intended to acquire an understanding of human relations, provide knowledge of basic principles and values of society, inculcate right attitudes, develop appropriate skills, teach tolerance, cultivate a forward outlook, impart mental training, help resolve contemporary, individual and social problems, foster national feelings and develop international understanding.

Edgar Bruce Wesley has rightly remarked, "The curriculum is an educational instrument, planned and used by the school to effect its purposes."

4.2 NEED FOR THE PLANNING OF CURRICULUM

The word '*curriculum*' is derived from the Latin word '*curresve*' which means to run. So curriculum is a course of path which one run to reach a goal. Thus curriculum includes the subject-matter and all learning experiences arranged by the school for a particular subject.

The needs of life go on changing so is education, so we cannot go on with a static curriculum. The content has to be selected according to the changing needs of the society in general and subject-matter in particular. The curriculum has to be planned and organised in a scientific manner keeping in view the psychological requirements of the students. If the curriculum is properly organised, it enables the students to know the subject-matter which they have to study. On the other hand it also makes clear to the teacher, the material that they have to teach to the students. It also provides the same facility to the examiner.

4.3 CONSTRUCTION OF CURRICULUM

The following two stages are important in the construction of curriculum:

(i) Selection of the curriculum, and

(ii) Organisation of curriculum material.

(i) Principles of Selection of the Curriculum

Tradition is not going to be our guiding principle in the selection and arrangement of the subject-matter. It is not possible or advisable to carry out the selection of a curriculum in a haphazard manner. Curriculum has to be properly planned and to be based on certain principles. There principles will be discussed now.

Principles of the Selection of Curriculum or Subject-matter

Though the organisation of various information and subject-material is a difficult task, yet educationists have tried to lay down certain principles, on the bases of which, the subject-material or the content material of civics may be organised. Some of these are as follow:

(a) Principle of Utility (or use)

Knowledge for the sake of knowledge is a good aim but in the existing circumstance it is not a successful aim. At present we have to keep in mind the utilitarian aspect of every subject-matter. If the subject-matter is not of any use the students will not feel interested in it for a long time. Thus the curriculum material should include only those topics which are useful for a particular grade in many ways. Firstly, an attempt be made to include those topics which are useful in day-to-day life. The curriculum material of the subject should have the following ingredients in it.

(i) It should be useful in every day life.

(ii) It should be useful in the study of other subjects.

(iii) It should have some vocational utility.

(iv) It should enable students to understand and appreciate the role played by civics in the development of civilization and other branches of knowledge.

(b) Principle of Disciplinary Value

Teaching of civics disciplines the mind. Previously this was the sole criterion to select the subject-matter. This brought into syllabus much useless material. The students used to study certain puzzles and riddles which had no practical utility. For disciplining the mind, one topic is as good as another. Unless and until is topic has some other values, it should not be included in the curriculum simply for its disciplinary value. Real useful problems train the mind better than unreal formal problems. When the students can get both useful knowledge and mental training from the same set of facts, it is not wise to make pupils learn one set of facts for mental exercise and another for the acquisition of knowledge. In the words of Thorndike, "Teach nothing merely because of its disciplinary value but teach everything so as to get, what disciplinary value it does have."

(c) Principle of Cultural Value

Civics has played an important role in the advancement of culture and civilisation. There may be certain ideas that were pursued by the students of civics which may not be of any use now. But there are certain ideas and facts of civics that form an integral part of modern culture and society. Such facts or ideas should be included in the curriculum. Their study will be a source of inspiration to the students.

(d) Principle of Preparatory Value

The material of the curriculum should be so selected that it should be prepatory as well as terminus. On the one hand, it should train the students for life and on the other it should also prepare them for higher education. The content should include the topics which prepare the child (i) for university education, (ii) for life. Only a small percentage of the students go up to the university stage and for most of them school is a terminal stage. Hence the requirements of college course need not dominate the school curriculum. After every stage of education some students enter life while others go in for higher education. The curriculum should be such as to be able to provide satisfactory education to both these categories of students.

(e) Principle of Child Centredness

Civics is a very vast subject so it becomes difficult to make a selection of the things which are useful to the students. For taking a decision about usefulness of the content material we should always keep in mind the child for whom it is meant. Do not forget that curriculum is for child and the child is not for the curriculum. While making a selection of useful topics for inclusion in curriculum childs' interests, abilities, age levels, etc., should be kept in mind. The duration of the course should also be given due consideration while making the selection of topics for inclusion in the curriculum. An attempt be made to provide in the curriculum topics for various categories of students.

(f) Principle of Community Centredness

Since every child has to live in and for the community, it would be desirable that he is able to live well in society. In the curriculum of civics all such topics be included which cater to the needs of the society. Thus an attempt be made to shape the curriculum according to the needs of the society.

(g) Principle of Flexibility

The aim of education as also the aims of teaching a subject go on changing because they depend on the needs of ever changing society. The developments in the subject also necessitate a change in curriculum. Thus it is not possible for us to follow any rigid curriculum forever. The curriculum has to be modified and reviewed quite frequently so as to shape it according to the latest developments of the subject. It is essential if we have to keep pace with the modern world. In this regards the views be sought from subject specialists.

(h) Principle of Activity

Educationists are of the view that 4 H's should find a place in the curriculum. In other words, it means that the content material should be based on these 4 H's. These H's are nothing but Health, Head, Hands and Heart. It means that a co-ordination should be established between the hands and the mind. Such a co-ordination would enable the children to act intelligently. Such activities should be given place in the curriculum that may lead to the activity of the children. Child is by nature active. His path of activity and agility should not be beset with difficulties. If it is beset with difficulties his progress will be retarded. The organisation and selection of the subject material of Civics should be based on activity. Such events, instances and topics of Civics should be included in the curriculum that lead to the activity in the child. The curriculum should also be so organised that it may bring about activity in the children.

(i) Principle of Utility

This is a world of selectivity. We follow the principle of pick choose in regard to subject material and activity. We take to activities and materials that are useful for our life and discard those that do not seem to be useful. Selection of that subject material of Civics shall be useful which fulfills our educational needs.

Whitehead has classified the educational life into three parts or stages—(1) Romance, (2) Precision, and (3) Generalisation.

Precision is nothing but utility. Selection of the subject material should be based on precision and utility. Material that is not precise and useful should not find a place in the teaching of Civics. By and by, with the development of various mental powers, the child is able to discriminate between useful and useless. He welcomes what is useful and discards what is not useful. If the content material of teaching is not based on the principle of utility, it shall not attract the students towards the study.

(j) Principle of Formality and Cultural Heritage

Every individual is proud of his or her cultural heritage. This is very true of India. We try to preserve the culture handed over to us by our forefathers. Alongwith it we also try to enrich it. This can be done if we include in the curriculum of teaching of Civics, the subject-material that helps preservation of culture and its enrichment. This is possible only if the subject-matter is selected on the basis of the principle of formality.

(k) Principle of Interest

In the modern education, interest, aptitude and other mental faculties play a vital role. Attempt is made to base the entire education in the interest of the children. In the teaching of Civics, such subject-material should be selected which is of interest to the students. Selection will not be sufficient. It should be so organised that it is interesting to the educands. If the content material is not based on interest, children shall not feel inclined to study it. The whole education today is child-centred. It is, therefore, all the more necessary, to organise the subject-material of the civics, with an eye on the interest of the child. In other words, the selection and organisation of the subject material should be according to nature of the child.

(l) Principle of Selectivity

We cannot have each and everything in the curriculum. We have to follow the principle of pick and choose. Those things that are helpful for the betterment of the society and bring about the preservation of the social values and cultural standards are given place in the curriculum. The content material should be so organised that it may help the students to understand social and political problems. The material should be in accordance with the intelligence and mental power of the students.

(m) Principle of Concentric Growth

This principle indicates that we should proceed 'from known to unknown' and 'from concrete to abstract'. First of all, those facts should be presented before the child that are already known to him. Then facts unknown to him should be presented before him and they should be connected with the known facts. This means that while teaching Civics, problems dealing with the local aspect of citizenship should be presented before the children. Then attempt should be made to present the national and international problems appertaining citizenship.

The child lives in the family. When he grows he comes in contact with his neighbourhood. Later on, he comes in contact with the town, the state, the country and the entire world. The knowledge and the teaching of Civics should begin with the knowledge of the family. First of all the teacher should try to present the citizenship before the child as it affects his family. By and by, he should go no broadening this circle of knowledge. It is in the end that the citizenship of the world or world citizenship should come before the student.

(n) Teachers' Points of View

While framing or revising the curriculum, the views of teachers, who are the real workers, should also be sought. They know the levels of students and the thing which should be taught to the students. At present, the curriculum is imposed on the teachers and as such, they do not realise the significance of changes in the curriculum if any. The new trend expects participation and contribution from the teachers side.

So we see while constructing curriculum for a grade, various considerations are to be kept in mind. Nothing should be included simply because of disciplinary value. Utility should provide the chief criterion of curriculum construction. Of course, the latest trends in the subject, the needs of community, the needs for students and above all, the views of the teachers should be given due weight in any scheme of curriculum construction.

View of J.W.A. Young in Regard to Selection of the Subject-matter of Curriculum

According to Young, selection of subject-matter of curriculum should be guided by the following consideration (or principles).

1. To exhibit most clearly and to the best advantages the various political thoughts.
2. To help to a better understanding of society.
3. To bring out clearly the relationships between civics and modern life and to show how civics can help to solve various problems of life.
4. To allow the organisation of material into a homogeneous whole, meeting the demands of pedagogy.

4.4 ORGANISATION OF CURRICULUM

Organisation of the Facts or Subject-matter

The second problem that we have to face in constructing curriculum or laying down the subject-material of teaching Civics is the Organisation of the facts. The facts should be so organised that the students may acquire them and assimilate them thoroughly. For this, various principles have been laid down. Some of these are as follows:

1. Psychological and Logical Arrangement

Logical arrangement leads to the rigorous treatment of the subject-matter which is based on logical reasoning whereas psychological arrangement is from the point of view of the students. It seems that both the approaches are different but these can be easily merged. The organisation can both the psychological and logical All thinking is psychological. Psychological throws light on the power of understanding of students at a particular stage. We can be logical in various ways. Psychological should decide which logical approach will suit for a particular topic. Logic will help in maintaining proper sequence of topics, so we should organise the topics in such a way that we may follow Psychological and Logic at the same time. The happy combination of the two is always desirable.

Psychological throws light on the use of a topic for the pupil from the academic as well as practical point of view. It takes into consideration the power of grasping and understanding of pupils in a particular age group. The order in which topics ar to be taken up will largely depend on its findings. Similarly logic must be there. Psychological should decide what kind of logic is appropriate for the pupil of a certain age and what type of topics will be suitable for the development of such logical thinking. Logic will help in maintaining the link and sequence of topics found useful and meaningful for the child.

Logical organisation of the subject-matter deals with the vigorous logical reasoning associated with the subjects.

2. Topical and Spiral Arrangement

Topical arrangement means that a topic should be finished entirely at one stage. It takes the topics as a unit. Spiral arrangement implies that a topic should be split up into different portions and these portions should be spread over different grades. Easier portions should be dealt with in the lower grades and the difficult portions should be gradually introduced in the next grade. The later is definitely a good arrangement. Topical arrangement requires that easy and difficult portions of a topic should be dealt with at one stage which is unpsychological.

However simple or easy topics may be finished at one stage, while spiral arrangement is good, long grinding at all grades is undesirable. The selection of a particular approach will depend on the topic.

3. From Easy to Difficult

Organisation of the content material of the curriculum be done keeping in view the mental development and the capacities of the students. The easier topics should come first and difficult ones later on. However, we should bear in mind that what appears easy to the teacher, may not be easy to the students, so this is to seen from the point of view of the student. For this we have to keep in mind the mental level, capacities and age level of the students.

For any particular class only those topics be included in syllabus which are within the comprehension of the students.

4. Principle of Activity

The child likes activity and these days activity plays an important part in teaching of a subject-matter. Organisation of curriculum should not fail to suggest some practical work whereever it is possible. In lower classes those topics be included which put more emphasis on practical work. It helps in making clear various concepts in civics and thus help in developing a love for the subject.

Following activities be kept in mind while organising the subject-matter of curriculum:

(i) Personal and home activities.

(ii) Recreational activities.

(iii) Vocational activities.

(iv) Community, civic and social activities.

(v) National activities.

5. Principle of Correlation

While organising the content in civics the principle of correlation should always be given due weightage. Correlation may be of different varieties. The following types of correlation must be kept in mind while organising curriculum in civics.

(i) Correlation of civics with the problems of every day life.

(ii) Correlation of civics with other subjects.

(iii) Correlation between different branches of social sciences.
(iv) Correlation with craft or work experience.

For correlating subject-matter we must know the following:

(i) Day-to-day life activities of the students.
(ii) The nature of topics included in other subjects at the same stage.
(iii) The sequence of topics of the same branch of the subject.
(iv) The nature of work experience or project undertaken by the students.

6. Scope of Individual Teaching

Psychology show that no two children are like. There are individual differences in students. The same type of rigid syllabus may not suit all the students. There may be ability grouping of students i.e., the students of almost the same intelligence and achievement may be but in one group. Accordingly there should be grouping of topics in the curriculum. There should be different assignments for bright and dull students.

The most prevalent view at present is that the requirements of the groups as a whole should have priority over individual requirements. However Educationist differ in this regard and some of them emphasise that the subject-matter of the curriculum should be so arranged that the difference in the abilities of students are not neglected.

7. Voice of the Teacher

The teacher must have definite say in the selection and organisation of the curriculum in civics. The teacher is the real field worker, who knows what is most suitable and where. At present, the teacher is not consulted at all. The curriculum is laid down for him. He is to faithfully go through it, without any alteration or modification.

8. Some other Requirements

(a) *Child centred Syllabus*. The curriculum should be child centred and not subject or topic-centred. Unless the requirement of the child are kept in view, the curriculum shall not be useful.

(b) *From Impirical to Rational*. The curriculum should be so organised that the students are able to acquire facts through experience, intuitions and induction. They should also be gradually made to feel the need for and appreciate the usefulness of deduction system of education. This method is known as the method of proceeding from impirical to rational. In other words, it means that the students should be made to proceed from known to unknown or from particular to general.

(c) *From Concrete to Abstract.* The curriculum should provide for the teaching of the subject on the principle of proceeding from concrete to abstract.

4.5 CURRICULUM OF CIVICS FOR VARIOUS STAGES OF EDUCATION

Normally speaking, we have five stage of education. These are:

(i) Pre-primary.

(ii) Primary.

(iii) Junior High School (Middle)

(iv) Secondary/Senior Secondary.

(v) University.

There is a need to have a properly organised curriculum of various stages of education. Outline syllabus for various stages is given below:

Syllabus or Curriculum at the Pre-primary and Primary Stage of Education

This is the stage where the children between the age of 4 to 11 years come for education. This education runs up to Class V. At this stage of education the main aim is to develop in the students the basic qualities of human life. The syllabus of Civics for this stage of education should be of an elementary nature. It should be based on certain elementary principles of formation of good habits and imparting knowledge of necessary requirements of life.

Prayer, healthy living, knowledge about school, festivals of social and cultural importance, gardening, knowledge about crops, postal facilities life in the locality, important places of cultural and educational, value should form the subject-material of the civics.

Curriculum Approach at the Primary Stages

The Curriculum for Ten Years (1976) has observed that the primary concern of the school at this stage should be to develop the necessary social skills, values and attitudes that would enable the child to contribute his mite, as he grows, towards the development of the society to which he belongs.

During the five years or primary school the child's mental horizon would be gradually widened from the home to the school and the local community to the world. In the process, the child would begin to appreciate the geographical elements of his environment. Various human activities, which help him to understand how the gifts of nature are processed to produce goods for serving the various needs of man, would also be studied. He would also get an idea of the social and cultural life in different parts of the country as well as of some different ways of living, in certain parts of the world. Stories and narratives about personages and events that have contributed to our national heritage and human heritage will also studied. In addition to these, the child would get ample opportunities to develop socially desirable habits, attitudes and values besides becoming broadly acquainted with the functioning of political and social institutions.

Curriculum Approach at the Middle and High School Stage

For the organisation of content in social sciences, comprising history, geography, civics and economics, in the next two stages of school education, three different approaches can be visualised.

History, geography and civics may be introduced as separate discipline in the middle classes and carried over as such to high school classes, while economics may be introduced at the high school stages as a separate discipline.

History and civics may form one group and geography and economics another group, and these two groups may be introduced right in Class VI and carried up to Class X.

The content of history, geography, civics and economics may be identified in an integrated manner for all the five years taken together.

While the first two approaches are common today and do not need any elaboration, except that they contribute to the isolation of the disciplines amongst themselves and of disciplines from problems of situations, in the third approach, it would be necessary to identify essential units in each subject in two cycles of three years and two years. The units thus identified for the first cycle of three years may be integrated and arranged sequentially between and within subjects in the form of a common syllabus for social science. For the next two years of education, a similar exercise may be done treating the earlier cycle as the base. Some old units may be taken at a greater depth while new ones may be introduced in each subject so as to lead to a slightly more advanced integrated syllabus in these subjects. While selecting units from individual subjects, care may be taken to preserve the general structure of the discipline and include those facts and principles which are useful to a growing adolescent and serve as a base for a systematic study of the subject subsequently.

Objectives of Teaching Civics in Middle Classes

The course in civics has the major responsibility of promoting well-informed and intelligent citizens who have the ability to participate in the affairs of their community effectively. From his point of view, the course at this stage aims mainly at imparting training in civic life rather than more scholarship. It contains such socially imperative knowledge which would not only impart understanding of the civic processes but would also provide training in the development of civic competencies. Some practical aspects of citizenship education have also been incorporated from the point of view of adopting a functional approach. Thus, the syllabus in civics at the middle stage has the following objectives:

1. To provide the student with intelligent understanding of the various social responsibilities and civic processes.
2. To help the student understand our Constitution and the values enshrined in it.
3. To acquaint the student with the machinery of the government at different levels.
4. To make the student conscious of the actual problems that are facing our country today and instil in him a sense or responsibility towards the community.

5. To make the student identify with the people and their institutions.
6. To inculcate in the student the values of democracy, secularism, socialism and national integration.

Curriculum Approach to Civics in Middle Classes

The course envisages the study of local government and the Indian Constitution in Classes VI and VII, respectively; and in the last year, i.e. in Class VIII, the students would study the actual problems that are facing India today. In the course, some practical aspects of citizenship education and the elements of economics should also be incorporated to adopt a functional and integrated approach.

Though many of the activities and topics of study included under this scheme may be organised by the teacher in the class or school, it is suggested that the training would be more fruitful if the students are taken out of the classroom and involved in real life situations.

Syllabus at the Junior High School Stage of Education

Here the course is of three years. The aim of education is to bring about the development of the physical and mental faculties of the students. A tendency to acquire knowledge and make discoveries about things is developing in the students. An attempt is made to integrate the teaching of Civics with the teaching of other subjects. Attempt is also made to teach the practical aspect of the Civics. The principles of Civics can very well be applied in the school life. The students can also be shown the working of the theory in the world outside the school. In fact the real aim of teaching Civics is to help the students to understand the elements of their social atmosphere, local life and their (political and cultural) aspect of the society. The syllabus of the Junior High Schools in Haryana is as given bellow:

1. Syllabus for Class VI

We have the following things in the syllabus:-

(i) The structure of the local administration—(a) towns, and (b) districts.

(ii) Organisation and functions of the Gram Sabhas and Gram Panchayats, their problems and the solutions of those problems.

(iii) Organisation and functions of the Municipalities and Zila Parishads.

(iv) National and local festivals.

Practical Works. Besides theoretical knowledge, the students are also expected to do the practical work. It includes the following:

(i) Organisation of the social service in the village or the town, sanitation and health of the town, drinking water, roads and measures for preventing the spread of diseases.

(ii) Celebration of national and local festivals and functions in the schools.

(iii) Celebration of the days of national importance such as Republic Day, Independence day, Gandhi Jayanti, Nehru Birthday etc.

2. Syllabus of Class VII

It includes the theoretical knowledge of the following:-

(i) The study of the working of the following: (a) Governor, (b) Cabinet, and (c) Legislature.

(ii) Study of the structure of the administration of various States of India, with special reference to Utter Pradesh.

(iii) Elections and franchise.

(iv) Structure of the judiciary in the court with special study of the following:

(a) Supreme court, (b) High court, and (c) Other sub-ordinate courts.

(v) Problems of the social life of the country such as educational problems.

(vi) Problems of untouchability, poverty, indebtedness, agricultural problems, economic problems and other social problems.

Practical Works. The theoretical knowledge of the students has to be given a practical shape. It can be done by employing the following measures:

(i) Continuance of the work started in class VI.

(ii) By practising the election system in the various bodies of the schools and the Unions.

(iii) Practising the principles of co-operation in the schools. This may be done by organising co-operative stores in the schools.

(iv) The democratic way of life may be practised in schools. Various Committees of the students may be formed for the organisation and arrangement of various activities in the schools.

(v) Newspaper may be read collectively. A student may read the paper and other may listen to it.

(vi) Lectures on important topics may be arranged and organised.

3. Syllabus of Class VIII

The theoretical aspect of the syllabus includes the following:

(i) Study of the structure of administration of the Central Government of the Indian Republic.

(ii) Study of the political problems and the working of the political parties.

(iii) Study of the following organs of the Government of India:

(a) President, (b) Cabinet, and (c) Parliament.

(iv) The following agencies and organisations of international importance may the studied with reference to India:

(a) United Nations Organisation,

(b) United Nations Organisation and its various agencies and branches.

(v) Study of the influence of great men on the society, such as, Mahatma Gandhi, Rabindra Nath Tagore, Jawahar Lal Nehru, Arvind Ghosh etc.

(vi) Impact of scientific inventions and discoveries on the life of the society.

(vii) Impact of industrialisation on society and various other problems.

Practical Work. In this class also the theoretical knowledge of the students has to be given a practical shape. It can be done by taking up the following activities:

(i) Continuance of the practical work done in the previous classes. An attempt should be made to improve it.

(ii) Study Groups should be organised. The working of the Parliamentary Government may be taught by organising School Parliament or such other activities.

(iii) An attempt should be made to help the expansion of education.

By casting a glance at the syllabus, it becomes clear that at this stage of education an attempt is made to acquaint the students with the various political, social, religious and cultural problems of the society. The students are also taught to play their part of the solution of the these problems.

Syllabus at the Secondary Stage of Education

When the student reaches this stage of education he has already acquired some maturity. His mental powers such as imagination, reasoning, power of determination, etc. have developed by now. The students have also, by this time, learnt the art of shouldering the responsibilities. They now try to understand various social, political, religious, and cultural problems. These things need that the syllabus at this stage of education should be scientific and properly organised. It should be competent to develop the students into ideal citizens of democratic republic.

Aims and Objective of Teaching Civic at the Secondary Stage of Education

This stage of education includes four classes, IX, X, XI and XII. The teaching of civics should aim at the following:

(1) To develop the spirit of sacrifice, co-operation, love, etc. among the students so that they may try to lead the life of an ideal citizen.

(2) The students should be acquainted with the democratic system of government of the State. This shall encourage them to take interest in the working of the government.

(3) The student should be given an idea of the complex structure of the society and various social problems. They should be given an opportunity to observe various events and objects. Such a step will develop the spirit of patriotism in the students. This patriotism and nationalism shall be in co-existence with

internationalism.

(4) The students should be given a practical idea of the government, by practising it, on a miniature stage, in the school.

(5) An attempt should be made to acquaint the students with the problems, of the country. Qualities of national consciousness, emotional integration, co-operation, equality etc. should be developed in them.

Syllabus of the Civics at the First Two Years of the Secondary Stage of Education

At this stage of education there shall be two papers of civics. The syllabus of both these papers shall be as given below:

1. First Paper

Principles and theory of Civics. This paper shall include the following:

(i) *Citizenship:* Meaning, how is it acquired and how is it lost. Rights and duties of a citizen, obstacles in the path of an ideal citizenship.

(ii) Individual society and associations—Its various kinds.

(iii) *States:* Relationship of the citizen with the State, function of the state etc.

(iv) *Types of the Government:* Their definitions.

(v) Various organs of the Government and their organisation Legislature, Executive and Judiciary.

(vi) Law and Liberty.

2. Second Paper

This paper shall deal with citizenship and administration. It shall include the following:

(i) Fundamental rights of the citizen under the Constitutions.

(ii) State Government their structure and relationship with the Central Government.

(iii) Administration of the districts of the States-District and Divisional Officers and their powers and duties.

(iv) *Local administration:* Organisation and functions of the local bodies, Municipalities, Zila parishads, their organisation and functions.

(v) Rural administration or administration of the villages. Gram Panchayats, Gram Sabhas, etc. their organisation and functions.

Syllabus for the Last Two Years of Secondary Education i.e., Classes XI and XII

According to the prospectus of the Board of High School and Intermediate Education, classes shall include the following:

1. First Paper

Principle of Civics.

(i) Its meaning, subject, its scope and its relation with other social sciences, society, state and different types or communities.

(ii) State and individual—sovereignty, law, freedom and equality and rights.

(iii) Origin of state theory.

(iv) Functions of a state—Meaning of a welfare state.

(v) Types of administration, constitution—Their types and principles of their classification.

(a) Legislative—Voters, political organisations and public opinion, bicameral legislatures.

(b) Executive—Different forms and ways of appointment, relation with legislature.

(c) Judiciary—Appointment and its function, functions and importance of the modern judiciary.

(vi) *Citizenship*—Meaning how to acquire citizenship, it rights and duties, hurdles in the functioning of ideal citizenship.

(vii) Ideals of civil life— Patriotism, Nationality, Internationalism, World Government.

2. Second Paper

Indian Administration and Civic life. Indian Union and its constitution. Constitution of Union Government and its functions:

(a) Union Executive—(1) President—Appointment, right and functions, (2) Cabinet—Appointment and functions.

(b) Union Legislature—Parliament, Rajya Sabha, Lok Sabha—formation and rights.

Relation between the two houses and the Executive. Formation of state government and their functioning centrally administered territories also included—Administrative position and study of North-East border states and Nagaland inclusive of centrally administered areas.

(a) Executives of states—appointment, rights and functions.

(b) Legislatures of states—Legislative Assemblies—Organisation and rights.

Legislative Assembly—Organisation and Rights—Relation between the two houses and Executive.

Indian Judiciary—Supreme Court and its importance.

Judicial System in U.P.

Public Services in India—Their importance, and their work and Public Service Commissions, Local self-government and its importance:

(a) Municipalities, Corporations and Zila Parishads.

(b) Kshetra Samities, Gaon Sabhas, Panchayat and Panchayti Adalat.

(c) Co-operative societies and Community development schemes.

Movements for religious and social reformations in India and their effect on political and national life of the country.

National movement—Performance of the Indian National Congress and its importance.

Sectarian and communal movements. Political organisation in the country.

Indian economic life—(a) Farmer—His problems and rural life,

(b) Industry and urban life, (c) Need of planned financial set up: (d) Programme of national plans.

India and the world—As a member of the commonwealth and its place in it is a member of the UNO.

India and Asian Countries—Particularly in relation with Peoples Republic of China and Pakistan.

CBSE Syllabi and Courses in Civics for Classes XI and XII

Central Board of Secondary Education, New Delhi has prescribed the following Syllabi and Courses for All India Senior School Certificate Examination:

POLITICAL SCIENCE

CLASS XI

3 Hours *One Paper* *100 Marks*

Foundation of Political Science

Unit I. Meaning, scope and significance of political science. Meaning, scope and relationship with history, economics, sociology and ethics.

Unit II. Citizen and his rights and duties.

(i) Meaning of rights and duties.

(ii) Relation between rights and duties.

Unit III. Basic Concepts.

(a) Law.

(b) Liberty.

(c) Equality.

(d) Justice—social and economic.

Unit IV. Society, state and nations.

(a) Meaning of society, state and its attributes; state, society and their relationship; and meaning of a political system.

(b) State and associations.

(i) Definition and type of associations.

(ii) Problems of loyalties and their co-ordination.

(c) State and the citizens.

(i) State as an instrument of socio-economic change.

(ii) The sphere and limits of state activity.

Unit V. Some major contemporary political theories.

(a) Liberalism and democracy.

(b) Fascism.

(c) Socialism and its brands—Marxism and Communism.

Unit VI. State and Government.

(i) State and government.

(ii) Classification and forms of government.

(a) Unitary and federal.

(b) Democratic and dictatorial.

(c) Socialist.

Unit VII. Organs of government.

(i) Executive.

(a) Types of Executive—Parliamentary and Presidential.

(b) Functions.

(ii) Legislature.

(a) Types of Legislature—unicameral and bicameral

(b) Functions.

(iii) Judiciary.

(a) Organisation of Judiciary.

(b) Functions and importance.

(c) Independence of judiciary.

Unit VIII. Role of bureaucracy in the modern state.

(i) Recruitment

(ii) Distinction between political executive and permanent executive and their roles.

Unit IX. Electorate.

(i) Adult suffrage—universal franchise.

(ii) Systems of representation, direct and indirect election.

Unit X. Public opinion.

(i) Role and importance of public opinion in a democratic policy.

Unit XI. Party System.

(i) Political Parties—their function and importance.

(ii) Mono, bi and multi-party system.

(iii) The role of opposition.

Unit XII. Interest of Pressure Groups.

(i) Class, caste and their interest groups.

(ii) Their nature and functions.

Suggestive Project Work

Any one of the following:

(1) Study of election procedure with reference to the elections of the Village Panchayats or Municipal Committees or Legislative Assembly or Lok Sabha.

(2) Study of students council's elections.

(3) Study of the working of a post office or a police station or a rationing office of the nearby area.

(4) Elementary study of manifesto of a major political party of India.

(5) Organising a group visit to any nearby local body or state legislature and observing how matters of public importance are discussed and decisions are taken in regard to them.

(6) Organising a group visit to nearby judicial court and observing how cases are conducted and decided.

CLASS XII

3 Hours *One Paper* *100 Marks*

Indian Constitution and Government

Unit I. National Movement and the Indian Constitutional Development.

(i) British imperialism and the national awakening.

(ii) Major phases of the Indian national movement and the

subsequent constitutional developments.

Unit II. Basic Principles of Indian Constitution.

(i) Preamble and salient features of the Indian Constitution.

(ii) Procedure of amendments in the Constitution.

Unit III. Fundamental Rights and Directive Principles of State Policy.

(i) Fundamental Rights.

(each category of right should be explained with apt illustrations).

(a) Guarantees provided in the Indian Constitution for the protection of the rights.

(b) Directive Principles of State Policy, importance and sanction behind them.

(i) Distinction and relationship between fundamental rights and directive principles.

(ii) Fundamental duties.

Unit IV. Indian Federal System.

(i) Indian federal structure.

(ii) Union and state relations.

Unit V. Union Government.

(i) The Union Executive; President and Council of Ministers.

(ii) The Union Legislature; Lok Sabha and Rajya Sabha.

Unit VI. The State Government.

(i) State Executive—Governor and Council of Ministers.

(ii) State Legislature—Vidhan Sabha and Vidhan Parishad.

(iii) Union Territories and their administration.

Unit VII. Indian Judicial Systems.

(i) Supreme Court.

(ii) High Court.

Unit VIII. Civil Services.

(i) Recruitment—UPSC and State Public Service Commissions.

(ii) The role of civil services.

Unit IX. Socio-Economic Factors Conditioning Indian Democracy.

Social and economic inequality, poverty, illiteracy and unemployment.

Casteism—untouchability, communalism, regional imbalances, feudal values and social tension.

Unit X. Democracy at Grassroots.

(i) Concept of Panchayati Raj.

(ii) Structure and working of Panchayati Raj.

(iii) Local bodies in urban areas.

Unit XI. Party System in India.

(i) Nature of party systems in India.

(ii) Study of major political parties.

(iii) Problems facing the party system.

Unit XII. Electoral System.

(i) Adult Franchise and Democratic Participation.

(ii) Election Commission and Election Procedure.

Unit XIII. India and the World.

(i) Bases and principles of Indian Foreign Policy.

(ii) India's relationship with her neighbours and big powers.

Evaluation of the Curriculum in Civics and Political Science

For Class VI to VIII. 1. The topics given broadly cover the instructional objects.

2. The number of topics adequate enough for each class considering the allotment of time.

3. The sub-topics included under each topics provide adequate coverage in respect of subject-matter for the concerned class.

4. The ideas given in the sub-topics are quite explanatory.

5. The language of topics and sub-topics is quite clear.

6. The topics included in each class give appropriate idea of the depth of treatment of topics to the users of the curriculum.

7. The concepts included in the curriculum are appropriate to the age-group and mental maturity of the children.

8. The sequencing of topics in the curriculum of middle stage (Class VI-VIII) is logical.

9. The sequencing to topics listed in the curriculum of each class is logical.

10. There is sufficient flexibility in the curriculum and a scope for considerable initiative on the part of the teacher.

For Class XII. 1. The curriculum includes some topics that introduce the student with the basic elements of sociology.

2. The topics included in each class appropriate idea of the depth of treatment of topics to the users of the curriculum.

3. The sub-topics included under each topic provide adequate coverage in respect of subject-matter for the concerned class.

4. The ideas given in the sub-topics are quite explanatory.

5. The language of topics and sub-topics is quite clear.

6. The concepts included in the curriculum are appropriate to the age-group and mental maturity of the children.

7. The sequencing of topics in the curriculum of Class IX to XII is logical.

8. The sequencing of topics listed in the curriculum of each class is appropriate.

9. There is sufficient flexibility in the curriculum and scope for considerable initiative on the part of the teacher.

10. The topics included in the curriculum tend to promote secularism, democracy and other Indian values wherever possible.

Revision Questions

1. What place would you give to civics is the Junior and senior high school syllabus ? Draw up briefly a syllabus for the same.
2. What do you understand by the term '*curriculum*'? What is the

need of the planning of curriculum ?

3. What are the various principles for selection of curriculum in civics ?

4. How is curriculum of civics organised ?

5. Critically examine the syllabus of civics at the middle stage of education.

6. Critically examine the CBSE syllabus in civics for Class XI and XII.

Chapter 5

Methods of Teaching Civics

5.1 INTRODUCTION

A *teaching method* is nothing but a way of importing knowledge to the students.

For teacher of every subject method is important. Method is nothing but a *scientific way of presenting the subject, keeping in mind the psychological and physical requirements of the children*. There may be more than one method of teaching, as there are more then one road for going to a destination. We have to select a method out of various methods of teaching. While selecting a method we have to keep in mind the psychology of the students, their interests, mental aptitudes and other mental faculties. In civics we make an effort to acquaint the child with the basic elements of ideal citizenship. In order to help the students to attain this goal, various methods are employed. It has rightly been said—

> "Methodology should be conceived as a dynamic function of education and not as a static aspect of the process of teaching."
>
> *Bining and Bining*

To quote the Secondary Education Commission, "Any method, good or bad links up the teacher and his pupils into an organic relationship with constant mutual interaction; It reacts not only on the mind of the students but on their entire personality; their standard of work and judgement, their intellectual and emotional development, their attitudes and values. Good methods which are psychologically and socially sound may raise the whole quality of life; bad methods debase it. So, in the choice and assessment of methods, teachers must always take into consideration their end products, namely the attitudes and values inculcated in them consciously and unconsciously."

Further emphasising the need for right methods, the Secondary

Education Commission states, "Every teacher and educationist or experience knowns that even the best curriculum and the most perfect syllabus remain dead unless quickened into life by he right method of teaching and the right kind of teacher. Sometimes even an unsatisfactory and unimaginative syllabus can be made interesting and significant by the gifted teacher who does not focus his mind of the subject matter to be taught or the information to the imparted but on his students—their interests and aptitudes, their reaction and response. He judges the success of his lesson not by the amount of matter covered but by the understanding, the appreciation and the efficiency achieved by the students."

In order to make children learn effectively the teacher has to adopt the right method of teaching.

5.2 VARIOUS METHODS OF TEACHING CIVICS

With the development of the subject-matter and knowledge of civics, various methods have evolved and are used for teaching of civics. Some of the important methods of teaching of civics are:

(1) Text-book Method;

(2) Lecture Method;

(3) Observation Method;

(4) Discussion Method;

(5) Project Method;

(6) Unit Method;

(7) Laboratory Method;

(8) Recitation or Socialised Recitation Method;

(9) Survey Method;

(10) Dramatic Method;

(11) Comparative Method; and

(12) Narration Method or Method or Narration.

(13) Activity Method.

Important Characteristics of a Good Teaching Method

1. They should aim to inculcating 'love of work'.

2. They should aim to develop the desire for doing work with the highest measure of efficiency of which one is capable. The motto of every school and its pupils should be "everything that is worth doing at all is worth doing well." Whether it be making a speech, writing a composition, drawing a map, cleaning the classroom, making a book rack or forming a queue.

3. They should provide various opportunities of free participation in accepted projects and activities wherein discipline and co-operation are constantly in demand.

4. They should aim at developing the capacity for 'clear-thinking' which distinguishes every truly educated person, "whether a student is asked to make a speech in a debating society or to write an essay or to answer a question in history, geography, or science or to experiment, the accent should always be on clear thinking and on lucid expression which is a mirror of clear thought."

5. The methods of teaching should expand the range of students interest. "We would urge all schools to provide in the time-table, at least one free period every day in which student may pursue their favourite hobbies and creative activities individually or in groups, preferably under the guidance of some interested teacher," recommended the Secondary Education Commission.

6. They should aim at providing opportunities to pupils to apply practically the knowledge that has been acquired by them. They should aim at transforming present bookish schools into work "schools" or "activity schools."

7. They should aim at the quickening of interest and training in efficient techniques of learning and study.

8. They should train the students in the art of study. They should train the students in the use of reference material such as the list of contents and index in books, the dictionary, the atlas, and reference books like the encyclopaedia.

9. They should be adapted to suit different levels of intelligence.

10. They should be such as they balance the claim of individual work with co-operative or group effort. The training of emotions, attitudes and

social capacities take place best in the context of projects and units of work undertaken co-operatively. The Secondary Education Commission has recommended that the teachers should be so trained that they are able to visualise and organise at least a part of the curriculum in the form of projects and activity-units which groups of students may take up and carry to completion.

We now take up a few of these methods:

1. Text-book Method

This is the method in which Civics is taught through text-books. Certain text-books are prescried for the students. The teacher teachers Civics on the basis of those text books. It is more or less a direct method of teaching Civics. This method is being used in India for a long time. It cannot be called independent method. The teacher and taught both are bound down by the limitations of the text-book. According to E.B. Weslay it is an old method of teaching and the Text-book method may be defined as that teaching procedure in which in understanding of the main body of information in the text-book is the immediate objective. It has certain advantages as well as disadvantages.

Merits of Text-book Method

(i) It brings about efficiency and provides knowledge to the students. The text-books are written with the students in view and so they are useful for them. They develop in the students the habit of study as well as self-study.

(ii) They develop in the students the habit of doing work in a systematic and scientific manner. Books are written in a scientific and systematised manner and so it is possible for the students to have an idea of a systematic works.

(iii) Since the students have to memorise the facts that are given in the books, their memory improves. Here Thorndike's law of learning operates.

2. Limitations of Text-book Method

(i) This method does not employ or use the maxims and principles of education.

(ii) This method narrows the outlook of students and they become inactive and lethargic. They do not participate actively in the acquisition of knowledge.

(iii) In the method the scope of revision is very limited and the knowledge acquired by the students is not permanent.

2. Lecture Method

Lecture method is the most commonly used method of teaching civics. This method is most commonly followed in colleges and in schools for teaching civics to higher classes. It is also known as 'Telling Method'.

In this method only the teacher talks and the students are the passive listeners. Since students do not actively participate in this method of teaching so this method is a teacher controlled and information centred. In this method teacher works as a sole resource is classroom instructions. Due to lack of participation students get bored and sometimes may go to sleep. In this method student is provided with readymade knowledge by the teacher and due to this spoon feeding the students loses interest and his power of reasoning and observation get no stimulus.

In this method teacher goes ahead with the subject-matter at his own speed. The teacher may make use of black-boards at times, and may also dictate notes. This teacher oriented method in its extreme form does not expect any questions or response from the students.

Advantages of Lecture Method

It has the following advantages:

(i) It is quite economical method. It is possible to handle a large number of students at a time and no laboratory equipment, aids, materials are required.

(ii) Using this method the knowledge can be imparted to the students quickly and the prescribed syllabus can be covered in short time.

(iii) It is quite attractive and easy to follow. Using this method teacher feels secure and satisfied.

(iv) It simplifies the task of the teacher as he dominates the lesson for 70-85% of lesson time and students just listen to him

(v) Using this method it is quite easy to impart factual information and historical anecdotes.

(vi) By following this method teacher can develop his own style of teaching and exposition.

(vii) In this method teacher can easily maintain the logical sequence of the subject by planning his lectures in advance. It minimises the chances of any gaps or overlappings.

(viii) Some good lectures delivered by the teacher motivate, instigate, inspire a student for some creative thinking.

Disadvantages of Lecture Method

The disadvantages of lecture method can be as under:

(i) In this method the students participation is negligible and students become passive recipients of information.

(ii) In this method we are never sure if the students are concentrating and understanding the subject matter being taught to them by the teacher.

(iii) In this method knowledge is imparted so rapidly that weak students develop a hatred for learning.

(iv) It does not allow all the faculties of the student to develop.

(v) In this method there is no place of 'learning by doing'.

(vi) It does not take into account the previous knowledge of the student.

(vii) It does not provide for corrective feedback and remedial help to slow learners.

(viii) It does not cater to the individual needs and differences of students.

(ix) It does not keep to inculcate scientific attitudes and training in scientific method among the pupils.

(x) It is an undemocratic and authoritarian method in which students depend only on the authority of the teacher. They cannot challenge or question the verdict of the teacher. This checks the development of power of critical thinking and proper reasoning in the student.

Conclusion

After considering various merits and demerits of method it may be concluded that this method may be suitable for teaching in higher classes (XI, XII) where we aim to cover the prescribed syllabus quickly. In these classes this method can be used successfully for imparting factual knowledge, introducing some new and difficult topics, make generalisation from the facts already known to the students, revision of lessons already learnt etc.

Teaching by this method the students of class XI and XII will also help those students who intend to join college so that they can prepare themselves for college where lecture method of teaching is a dominant method of imparting instructions.

This method of teaching can be made more beneficial if the teacher encourages his students to take notes during the lesson. After the lesson teacher can give to his students some-time for asking questions and answer their questions without any hesitation. While delivering his lesson the teacher may see that the lesson in delivered in good tone, loudly and clearly. He should use only simple and understandable words for delivering his lesson. If teacher can introduce some humour in his lesson it would keep students interested in his lesson.

3. Observation Method

Students travel from one place to another during tours and while going from one place to another they get an opportunity to observe and see things for themselves. A real impression of an object or a place can best be gained through personal observation. Direct experience is an essential step to right understanding. If the students are given an opportunity to acquire knowledge of civics by observing things themselves the knowledge shall be stable and shall have a practical value. The knowledge acquired through this method is clear, complete and perfect.

It is most desirable that observational work of the pupils be carefully directed and guided by the teacher. The students in lower classes may be asked to observe various things in their environment, near their homes, village and such other localities. They may be told to collect the relevant data. This data will help them understand similar conditions in their own provinces extending to other countries of the world. The observation method has a very wide range and can be very conveniently employed. The teacher does not play any part in this method. He remains a guide and a philosopher. No doubt he encourages the students to acquire knowledge.

This method may be used at any stage of education, best it is quite useful at primary and secondary stages of education.

Some of the important requirements of this method are as under:

(i) The teacher himself should have properly observed and seen things which he expects his students to see and observe. It is important because in the absence of a thorough knowledge of those things he will not be able to impart as scientific knowledge to his students.

(ii) Necessary data must be collected during observation.

Merits of the Observation Method

It has the following qualities in it:

(i) Here the students acquire knowledge independently. They remain active in the acquisition of knowledge and so the knowledge that is acquired, is stable and stands is good stead in future life.

(ii) This lead to the development of mental faculties of observation, reasoning, thinking etc.

(iii) It brings about a close co-operation in the school and the society.

(iv) The knowledge that is acquired by this method is acquired directly by the child.

Difficulties of the Method

(i) While on trips/tours the teacher sometimes has to face the problem of discipline.

(ii) The tours/trips cannot be planned to observe things that are situated far away.

(iii) Sometimes guardians are reluctant to permit their words to go out for observation.

Precautions

Teacher, if he wants to use this method, should keep the following things in his mind:

(i) Here the teacher asks his students to observe a thing, he should himself observe it. This will help the teacher to guide his students properly.

(ii) The teacher should act as an alert guide. No doubt, students should be given freedom to observe things but while giving them freedom, he should keep an eye on them so that they may not go astray.

(iii) Observation should not be passive. The teacher should continue to ask questions to the students so that they may go on understanding the things that they have observed.

(iv) The task of the teacher does not finish with the observation. He should test whether the students have really acquired knowledge or not.

(v) The teacher should try to ask the students to write down what they have observed. This will give a stable base to the knowledge.

4. Discussion and Debate Method

This method is said to be very useful for the study of social sciences. In this method the students are given certain problems and they are asked to discuss and debate them. They are themselves asked to prepare the outline of the discussions. Students prepare the discussions at home and they study the problems thoroughly well. This discussion may be on formal as well as informed lines. In this method the students get opportunity to express their ideas and feelings independently.

Merits of Discussion and Debate Method

(i) In this method, the students are faced with the problems, as they shall have to face in life.

(ii) By this method the defects of the classroom teaching may be removed and the students may be made active partners in the process of the education.

(iii) In this method the students themselves acquire knowledge and so the knowledge is stable and permanent.

(iv) This gives a chance to the students to solve their personal and individual problems. They learn a practical way of life.

(v) It leads to the development of the mental faculties of thinking, reasoning, determination, etc.

(vi) In discussion, the students have to present their ideas in a systematic manner. In doing so, they learn the art of systematising and organising their ideals properly. This is a great boon for future life.

5. Project Method

This method was given by Dewey—the American philosopher, psychologist and practical teacher. The project method is a direct outcome of his philosophy. According to Dr. Kilpatrick, "A project is a unit of whole hearted purposeful activity carried on preferably, in its natural setting." According to Stevenson "A project is a problematic act carried to its completion in its natural setting." According to Ballard, "A project is a bit of real life that has been incorporated into the school."

The project method is not totally new. Project equivalents are advocated for the adolescent period by Rousseau in Emile (BK-III). A project plan is modified form of an old method called "concentration-of-studies." The main features of "concentration-of-studies plan" is that some subject is taken the core or centre and all other school subjects as they arise are studied in connection with it.

Project method is based on the following principles:

(i) Learning by doing.

(ii) Learning by living.

(iii) Children learn better through association, co-operation and activity.

In this method, a project is taken, which is then completed in a natural and social setting. As the project is carried to completion, the students learn so many things.

Procedure

Project method generally involves the following steps:

(i) *Providing a situation.* The teacher provides a situation wherein the students feel like working on certain projects.

(ii) *Choosing*. Then the pupils are helped to choose a project linked to their need.

(iii) *Planning*. Pupils then discuss how that project is to be executed ? Steps of the procedure are planned and noted down.

(iv) *Executing*. The project is then executed as planned. Every body contributes his share of work.

(v) *Evaluating*. The project is then evaluated and the possible knowledge is reviewed.

(vi) *Recording*. The knowledge gained is then recorded for future reference.

What is an Educational Project ?

Various definitions of project have already been considered. A modified definition of project is given by Tomas and Long. They define it as "a voluntary undertaking which involves constructive effort or thought and eventuates into objective results."

Considering various definitions of project we may consider it as a kind of life experience which is an outcome of a craving or desire of the pupils. This is a method of spontaneous and incidental teaching. "Learning by living" may be a better meaning of project method, because life is full of projects and individuals carry out these projects in their every day life.

The projects may broadly be classified as—

(i) Individual projects, and

(ii) Social projects.

Individual projects are to be carried out by individuals whereas social projects are carried out by a group individuals.

Steps in a Project

For completing a project we have five stages in actual practice. These are—

(i) Providing a situation

(ii) Choosing and proposing.

(iii) Planning of the project.

(iv) Executing the project.

(v) Judging the project.

Recording the project is also essential.

(i) Providing a Situation

A project should arise out of a need felt by pupils and it should never be forced on them. It should be purposeful and significant. It should look important and must be interesting. For this the teacher should always be on the look out to find situation that arise and discuss them with students to discover their interests. Situations may be provided by different methods. Some such methods may include talking to students on the topics of common interest e.g., how did they spend their holidays, what did they see in Delhi etc.

(ii) Choosing and Proposing

From various definitions of an educational project we get the same underlying ideas (a) school tasks are to be as real and as purposeful as the task of wider life beyond the school walls. (b) they are of such a nature that the pupils is genuinely eager to carry them out in order to achieve a desirable and clearly realised aim.

According to Kilpatrick, "the part of the pupils and the part of the teacher, in most of the school work, depends largely on who does the proposing." The teacher should refrain from proposing any project otherwise the whole purpose of the method would be defeated. Teacher should only tempt the students for a particular project by providing a situation but the proposal for the project should finally come from students. The teacher must exercise guidance in selection of the project and if the students make an unwise choice, the teacher should tactfully guide them for a better project. The essentials of a good project are:

(i) It should have evident worth for the individual or the group that undertakes them.

(ii) The project must have a bearing on a great number of subjects and the knowledge acquired through it may be applicable in a variety of ways.

(iii) The project should be timely.

(iv) The project should be challenging.

(v) The project should be feasible.

It is for the teacher to see that the purpose of the project is clearly defined and understood.

(iii) Planning

The students be encouraged by the teacher to plan out the details of the project. In the process of planning teacher has to act only as a guide and he should give suggestions at times but actual planning be left to the students.

(iv) Execution

One the project has been chosen and details of the project have been planned, the teacher should help the students in executing the project according to the plan. Since execution of a project is the longest step in project method so it needs a lot of patience on the part of the students and the teacher. During this step the teacher should carefully supervise the pupils in manipulative skills to prevent waste of materials and to guard accidents. The teacher should assign work to different students in accordance with their tastes, interests, aptitudes and capabilities. Teacher should see that every member of the group gets a chance to do something. Teacher should constantly check up the relation between the chalked out plans and the developing project and as far as possible 'at the spot' changes and modification be avoided. However, if such changes become unavoidable these should be noted and reasons explained for future guidance.

(v) Evaluation

The evaluation of the project be done both by the pupils and the teacher. The pupils estimate the qualities of what they have done before the teacher gives his evaluation. The evaluation of the project has to be done in the light of plans, difficulties in the execution and achieved results. Let the students have self-criticism and look through their own failings and findings. The step is very useful because as a result of the project, the pupils can know the values of the information, interest, skills and attitudes that have been modified by the project.

(vi) Record

A complete record of the project be kept by the students. The record should include every-thing about the project. It should include the proposal, plan and its discussion, duties allotted to different students and how far were they carried out by them. It should also include the details of places visited and surveyed, maps etc., drawn, guidance for future and all other possible details.

Role of Teacher

(i) In project method of teaching the role of a teacher is that of a guide, friend and philosopher.

(ii) He helps the students in solving their problems just like an elder brother.

(iii) He encourages his students to work collectively, amicably in the group.

(iv) He also helps his students to avoid mistakes.

(v) He makes it a point that each member of the group contributes some thing to the completion of the project and in this process helps the shy and weaker students to work along with their class mates.

(vi) It the students face failure during execution of some steps of the project the teacher should not execute any portion of the project but should only explain to his students the reasons of their failure and should suggest them some better methods or techniques that may be used by them next time for the success of the project.

(vii) During the execution step teacher also learns something.

(viii) Teacher should always remain alert and active during execution, step and see that the project goes to completion successfully.

(ix) During execution of the project teacher should maintain a democratic atmosphere.

(x) Teacher must be well read and well informed so that he can help the students to the successful completion of the project.

Merits of the Project Method

(i) It is a method of teaching based on psychological laws of learning. The education is related to child's life and he acquires it through meaningful activity.

(ii) It imbibes the spirit of co-operation as it is a co-operative venture. Teacher and students join in the project.

(iii) It stimulates interest in natural as also man-made situations. Moreover the interest is spontaneous and not under any compulsions.

(iv) The method provides opportunities for pupils of different tastes and aptitudes with in the frame work of the same scheme.

(v) It upholds the dignity of labour.

(vi) It introduces democracy in education.

(vii) It brings about a close correlation between a particular activity and various subjects.

(viii) It is a problem solving method and places very less emphasis on cramming or memorising.

(ix) It helps to inculcate social discipline through joint activities of the teacher and the taught.

(x) A project can be used to arouse interest in a particular topic as it blends school life with outside world. It provides situations in which the students come in direct content with their environment.

(xi) It develops self-confidence and self-discipline.

(xii) A project tends to illustrate the real nature of the subject.

(xiii) A project affords opportunity to develop keenness and accuracy of observation and produces a spirit of enquiry.

(xiv) It puts a challenge to the student and thus stimulates constructive and creative thinking.

(xv) It provides the students an opportunity for mutual exchange of ideas.

(xvi) This method helps the children to organise their knowledge.

Drawbacks of the Project Method

(i) Projects require a lot of time.

(ii) Though the method provides the student superficial knowledge of so many things it provides insufficient knowledge of some fundamental principles.

(iii) In the project planning and execution of the project the teacher is required to put in much more work in comparison to other methods of teaching.

(iv) The teacher has been assumed as master of all subjects which is practically not possible.

(v) Good text books on these lines have not yet been produced.

(vi) It is an expensive method it involves tours, excursions, purchase of apparatus and equipment etc.

(vii) The method of organising instructions is unsystematised and thus the regular time table of work will be upset.

(viii) The method may fit those who cannot listen but it is very questionable if it has the same value for those who can listen.

(ix) The method leaves a gap in pupils knowledge.

(x) It underestimates man's power of imagination which enables him to savour the full experience of another without the necessary of undergoing the experience himself.

(xi) Sometimes the project may be too ambitious and beyond pupils capacity to accomplish.

(xii) Larger project in hands of an unexperienced teacher lead to boredom.

(xiii) The education given by projects is likely to emphasise relationships in breadth than the depth.

Conclusion

The project method provides a practical approach to learning of both theoretical and practical problems. It it is difficult of follow this method of a teaching it would be better at least not to ignore the spirit of this method.

This method has been found to be more suitable for primary and middle classes and is of restricted use for high and higher secondary classes. This method may be tried alongwith formal classroom teaching without disturbing the school time-table. With this in view some projects may be undertaken by the students to be completed on certain fixed days of a week. Alternately first half of the day may be devoted to class room teaching and the project work be carried out in the remaining half day. To help solve the problem of fund's shortage such project be chosen which are self-supporting. As it is not suitable for drill and continuous and systematic teaching. It is not very desirable to use it freely.

6. Unit Method

This method is of foreign origin and is quite popular in the United States of America. Gestalt's psychological theories have played a vital role in the development of this method. In this method it is proposed to present the subject-matter for teaching as a whole. This method is based on the assumption that body is a co-ordinated unit of physical and biological units. In the words of Henry. C. Mosrison: "Unit is a comprehensive and significant aspect of the environment of an organised science and an art. This is intended to make the teaching essay convenient. For the convenience of teaching, a subject-matter is divided into certain units."

Step of Unit. Morrison has laid down the following five steps of a unit:

(1) *Exploration.* Under this procedure the students are prepared for a new unit. An attempt is made to explore their past knowledge.

(2) *Presentation.* At this stage, the teacher through lecture and narration tries to present an outline of the unit to be presented before the students.

(3) *Assimilation.* Under this heading, the students try to own and acquire the information that is provided to them.

(4) *Recording.* At this stage the students try to organise the information that they have assimilated.

(5) *Recitation.* At this stage, the students try to express in form of a lecture or action that they have acquired.

These stages cannot be determined from before hand. They grow out of the contact between the students and the teacher.

Merits of the Unit Method

This method has the following merits:

(1) This creates interests in the students for the subject.

(2) It is based on the idea of giving whole knowledge to the students and tries to remove the shyness of the students.

(3) The students are taught to draw up plans of action. This drawing up of plans is helpful for their future life.

(4) It is based on individual differences and develops in the students the habit of self-study.

(5) The students are taught the lesson of carrying out their duties sincerely and shouldering the responsibilities properly.

(6) It develops, in the students, the qualities of sympathy, love, tolerance, leadership, discipline, etc.

Limitations of Unit Method

In spite of the merits present in this method certain critics have pointed out certain defects as well. They are being enumerated below:

(1) It is not useful for all subjects.

(2) It does not train the students in the art of appreciation and does not develop only the aesthetic quality.

(3) It is a very expensive method and consumes a lot of time.

(4) Since the method lays stress on imparting knowledge of the whole to the students, so either the students acquire a whole knowledge or do not acquire any knowledge at all.

7. Dalton Plan or Laboratory Method

Origin and Significant of Daltan Plan. This method was given by Miss Helen Parkurst but it is not named after her. It is named after the town where it was adopted for the first time for teaching in a high School. It is also called Laboratory Plan because writing about the importance of word, 'Laboratory', Miss H. Parkurst says, "I cling to it in the hope that it may gradually shift the educational point of view away from the atmosphere of prejudice which the word 'School' calls up in our mind. Let us think school rather as a sociological laboratory where the pupils themselves are the experiments, not the victim of an intricate and crystallised system in the evolution of which they have neither part nor lot. Let us think of it as a place where community conditions prevail as they prevail in life itself."

Principles Underlying Dalton Plan

This method of teaching is based on the following principles:

(i) The Principle of Individual Work

John Adams says, "It is the most dramatic and systematic break away from the class teaching unit." In this method equal opportunities are provided to each student to work at his own speed and rate. In this method it is not essential that equal time is taken by each student but it aims at the achievement of a minimum uniform standard. According to Miss H. Parkurst, "It is a piece of machinery for putting into operation the principle of individual work."

(ii) The Principle of Freedom

In this method of teaching there are no arbitrary fixed periods, there are no classroom restrictions or rigidity or discipline. In the words of a scholar, "It aims at giving to the older child that freedom for self-development which has proved so valuable in the school life of the infant while at the same time ensuring that he shall master thoroughly the academic work required by the curriculum of the school."

(iii) The Principle of Self Effort

In this method child gains knowledge through his own efforts.

(iv) The Principle of Co-operation

According to Miss H. Parkurst, " The school can only reflect the social experience of community when all its parts or groups develop the same intimate relations with one another as is found in socicty as a whole. The school should be organised in such a way as the pupils and teachers come in close interaction with one another." The students live and work together with the same teachers, in the same shared common workshops or laboratories.

(v) The Principle of Setting Goals

In this method a goal is set which provides a stimulus to the child to work in a way so as to attain the goal.

The plan works as under:

(i) Assignments or contracts. After the teacher has outlined the work to be completed during a year, he divides and sub-divides it into various units and then be prepares the assignments. While preparing the assignments teacher keeps in mind various factors such as holidays, time available, revision at various stages, curriculum activities and the demand of other subjects.

Each subject has its separate assignment and the student must complete his first assignment in each subject before proceeding to a second assignment in any subject. Moreover, he must complete all the assignments for a particular period in time.

(ii) Subject teachers. The student is guided and supervised by a subject teacher who is a specialist in his subject.

(iii) Subject rooms. Each specialist is incharge of his subject room that is equipped with the material needed in that subject. The student is free to came to the room and devote as much time as he likes in a particular subject room.

(iv) Records. To show the work done by each student graphs are maintained. They serve as a mirror of pupils work and also serve as a link between teacher and student. Such a graph is a contract remainder of the 'contract' or 'promise'.

(v) Conference. In afterroom session group discussions are arranged under the guidance of the teacher. Such discussions are known as 'conference' and these are devoted to remove common difficulties and also to explain certain items of common interest and importance.

Duties of a Teacher

Given below are some of the important duties of teacher in Dalton Plan:

(i) Preparation of assignments and giving them to the pupil as and when required.

(ii) Keeping an atmosphere of study in the room.

(iii) Giving explanations of any details of the assignment and removing the difficulties of the pupils.

(iv) Giving information with regard to the use of relevant equipment and materials.

(v) Ensuring the each assignment is finished properly before the new assignment is given to the pupil.

(vi) Keeping full records of the progress made by pupils in different classes.

(vii) Keeping the subject-library and other equipment up-to-date and in proper order.

The teacher, in the Dalton Plan, is "a helper, not a driver; the pursued, not the pursuer."

Merits of Plan

The plan has the following advantages:

(i) Individualised teaching.

(ii) Continuity of work.

(iii) Development of qualities such as self-effort and self-confidence.

(iv) Purposeful learning.

(v) Development of desirable study habits.

(vi) Development of a sense of responsibility.

(vii) Solving the problems of home-task.

(viii) Solving thc problem of discipline.

(ix) Simplification of the problem of evaluation.

(x) Better pupils-teacher relationship.

Limitations of the Method

(i) Not suitable for the average child and a shirker.

(ii) Development of individualistic tendencies .

(iii) Purely intellectual plan.

(iv) Unsuitable for a lesson that needs inspiration treatment.

(v) Lack of suitable teachers.

(vi) Lack of well-equipped libraries.

(vii) Unsuitable for junior classes.

(viii) Very costly.

(ix) No provision for individual differences.

8. Discussion Method

Discussion is totally different from *debate*. In *debate* the participant makes an all-out effort to prove a point whereas in *discussion* the participants try to discover the truth. Discussion stimulates the mental activity and helps in developing fluency and ease in expression. An exchange of ideas and opinions offers valuable training to students in reflective thinking.

Important Constituents of Discussion

Following are the important constituents:

(i) *The leader* — the teacher

(ii) *The group* — the class

(iii) *The problem* — the topics under discussion

(iv) *The content* — body of knowledge

(v) *Evaluation* — change in ideas, attitudes etc.

Directing Group Discussions

The teacher has to show immense patience and skill to ensure that discussion takes place on right lines and in the appropriate environment. Following points may be considered in this respect:

1. Students should be well-acquainted with the significance of the topic, its nature and scope and causes why the class should discuss it.
2. Discussion should be confined to important aspects.
3. Students should be encouraged to participate in the discussion.
4. Ideas may be invited without pressure or embarrassment.
5. Explanations, where needed, should be provided.
6. Personality cult should be avoided.
7. Co-operation rather than competition should be encouraged.
8. Efforts should be made to develop team spirit.
9. Doubts, mistakes and wrong interpretation should be made clear by the teacher.
10. Facts and points should be evaluated.
11. Facts and points should be summarised.
12. Students should be guided to honour difference of opinion and views.
13. Goals of discussions should be kept in view.
14. Only a few students should not be allowed to dominate class-room discussion.
15. Shy students may be given training in discussion is small groups so that their hesitation is removed while participating in bigger groups.

Organisation of Discussion

Following are the main techniques of organising a discussion.

1. Introducing a topic or a problem by the teacher by giving points or explanation to serve as the basis of discussion.
2. Calling upon a pupil by the teacher of give facts, describe a scene or situation, explain an incident, event of happening for getting the discussion started.
3. Preparing an outline of points co-operatively by the teacher and

a few students which may become the starting point for discussion.

4. Asking the students to describe their own experiences connected with the subject, topic or problem and making them points for discussion.
5. Presenting detailed papers by the teacher and discussions thereon.
6. Presenting detailed papers by the students and discussing them in the class.
7. Showing special works and projects to the class and discussing them.
8. Showing some pictures charts, diagrams or any audiovisual material and discussion about them.

Merits of Discussion

1. It helps in clarifying issues.
2. It helps children in crystallising their thinking.
3. It helps students in discovering what they do not know and what they have overlooked.
4. It engenders more reflection. It is farther from rote learning.
5. It represents a type of pooled knowledge, ideas and feelings of several persons.
6. It develops team spirit.
7. It engenders toleration of views which are at variance.
8. It affords opportunities to the students to learn together, make suggestions, share responsibility, comprehend the topic, evaluate the findings and to summarise results.
9. It provides opportunities to the students to speak distinctly, stand and sit correctly respect the ideas of others, share interests, ask pertinent questions and comprehend the problem before the group.
10. It helps the teacher in discovering talented students who have potential for becoming good leaders.

Limitations of Discussion

1. It is not suitable in all topics.
2. It is likely to be dominated by a few students.
3. It is likely to go off the track.
4. It may lead to unpleasant feelings.
5. It may create emotional tensions.
6. It may involve unnecessary arguments.

9. Heuristic Method

It is a pure discovery method. In Heuristic method, the student be put in the place of an independent discoverer. Thus no help or guidance is provided by the teacher in this method. In this method the teacher sets a problem for the students and then stands aside while they discover the answer.

In words of Professor Armstrong, "Heuristic methods of teaching are methods which involve out placing students as far as possible in the attitude of the discoverer—methods which involve their finding out instead of being merely told about things."

The method requires the student to solve a number of problems experimentally. To almost every one—especially children—experiments and science are synonymous. Once an idea occurs to a scientist he immediately thinks in terms of ways of trying out his ideas to see if he is correct. Trying to confirm or disprove something, or simply to test an idea, is the backbone of the experiment. Experiments start with questions in order to find answers, solve problems, clarify ideas or just to see what happens. Experimenting should be part of the elementary school science programme as an aid to helping children find solutions to science problems as well as for helping them to develop appreciation for one of the basic tools of science.

Procedure of the Method

The method requires the students to solve a number of problems experimentally. Each student is required to discover everything for himself and is to be told nothing. The students are led to discover facts with the help of experiments, apparatus and books. In this method the child behaves like a research scholar.

In the stage managed heuristic method, a problem sheet with minimum instructions is given to the student and he is required to perform the experiment concerning the problem in hand. He must follow the instructions, and enter in his notebook an account of what he has done and results arrived at. He must also put down his conclusion as to the bearing which the result has on the problem in hand. It his way he is led to reason from observation.

Essentially therefore, the heuristic method is intended to provide a training in method. Knowledge is a secondary consideration altogether. The method is formative rather than informational.

The procedures and skills in science problem solving can only be developed in classrooms where searching is encouraged, creative thinking is respected, and where it is safe to investigate, try out ideas, and even make mistakes.

Teachers Attitudes

One of the most important aspects of the problem solving approach to children's development in scientific thinking is the teachers attitude. His approach should be teaching science with a question mark instead of with an exclamation point. The acceptance of and the quest for unique solutions for the problem that the class is investigating should be a guiding principle in the teacher's approach to his programme of science. Teachers must develop sensitiveness to children and to the meaning of their behaviour. Teachers should be ready to accept any suggestion for the solution of problems regardless of how irrelevant it may seem to him, for this is really the true spirit of scientific problem solving. By testing various ideas it can be shown to the child that perhaps his suggestion was not in accord with the information available. It can then be shown that this failure gets us much closer to the correct solution by eliminating one possibility from many offered by the problem.

In this method teacher should avoid the temptation to tell the right answer to save time. The teacher should be convinced that road to scientific thinking takes time. Children should never be exposed to ridicule for their suggestions of possible answers otherwise they will show a strong tendency to stop suggestions.

For success of this method a teacher should act like a guide and should provide only that much guidance as is rightly needed by the student. He should be sympathetic and courteous and should be capable enough to plan and devise problems for investigation by pupils. He should be capable of good supervision and be able to train the pupils in a way that he himself becomes dispensable.

Merits of Heuristic Method

This method of teaching science has the following merits:

(i) It develops the habit of enquiry and investigation among students.

(ii) It develops habit of self-learning and self-direction.

(iii) It develops scientific attitudes among students by making them truthful and honest for they learn how to arrive at decisions by actual experimentations.

(iv) It is psychologically sound system of learning as it is based on the maximum, "learning by doing."

(v) It develops in the student a habit of diligency.

(vi) In this method most of the work is done in school and so the teacher has no worry to assign on check home task.

(vii) It provides scope for individual attention to be paid by the teacher and for close contacts. These contacts help in establishing cordial relations between the teacher and the taught.

Limitations of Heuristic Method

Main limitations of this method are as under:

(i) It is a long and time consuming method and so it becomes difficult to cover the prescribed syllabus in time.

(ii) It pre-supposes a very small class and gifted teacher and the method is too technical and scientific to be handled by an average teacher. The method expects of the teacher a great efficiency and hard work, experience and training.

(iii) There is tendency on the part of the teacher to emphasize those branches and part of the subject which lend themselves to heuristic treatment and to ignore important branches of the subject which do not involve measurement and quantitative work and are therefore not so suitable.

(iv) It is not suitable for beginners. In the early stages, the students needs enough guidance which if not given, may greatly disappoint them and it is possible that the child may develop a distaste for studies.

(v) In this method too much stress is placed on practical work which may lead a student to form a wrong idea of the nature of science as a whole. The grow up in the belief that science is something to be done in the laboratory, forgetting that laboratories were made for science and not science for laboratories.

(vi) The gradation of problems is difficult task which requires sufficient skill and training. The succession of exercises is rarely planned to fit into a general scheme for building up the subject completely.

(vii) Sometimes experiments are performed merely for sake of doing them.

(viii) Learning by this method, pupils leave school with little or no scientific appreciation of their physical environment. The romance of modern scientific discovery and invention remains out of picture for them and the humanizing influence of the subject has been kept away from them.

(ix) Evaluation of learning through heuristic method can be quite tedious.

(x) Presently enough teachers are not available for implementing learning by heuristic method.

Conclusion

This method cannot be successfully applied in primary classes but this method can be given a trial in secondary classes particularly in higher secondary classes. However, in the absence of gifted teachers, well-equipped laboratories and and libraries and other limitations this method has not been given a trial in our schools. Even if these limitations are removed this method may not prove much useful under the existing circumstances and prevailing rules and regulations. Though not recommending the use of heuristic method for teaching of science it may be suggested that at least a heuristic approach prevails for teaching of science in our schools. By heuristic approach we mean that students be not spoon fed or be given a dictation rather they be given opportunities to investigate, to think and work independently alongwith traditional way of teaching.

10. Problem Solving Method

In this method the student is required to solve a problem making use of his pervious knowledge. Problem solving may be defined as a planned attack upon a difficulty or perplexity in which a person makes use of his ability and capacity to find a suitable and satisfying solution. Yoakam and Simpson define it as, " A problem that occurs in a situation is which a felt difficulty is clearly present and recognised by the thinker. It is may be purely mental difficulty or it may be physical and may involve manipulation of data. The distinguishing thing about a problem, however, is that an individual who meets it as needing a solution, recognising it as a 'challenge'. It is a method in which some difficulty of act in an educational setting is felt and an attempt is make is a conscious planned and purposeful way to find its solution."

Dewey observes, " whenever—no matter how slight and common place is character—a difficulty perplexes and challenges the mind so that it makes belief at all uncertain—there is a genuine problem." He further ties problem solving with reflective thinking as follows, " The problem fixes the end of thought and the end controls the process of thinking."

According to Gates, "A problem exists for an individual when he has a definite goal and he cannot reach by the behaviours pattern which he already available."

Steps in Problem-Solving

Following are the important steps in problem-solving method:

(i) The formation and appreciation of the problem.

(ii) The collection of relevant data and material.

(iii) Organisation of data.

(iv) Drawing of conclusions.

(v) Testing conclusions.

Teacher's Role in Problem Solving Method

Quoting Professor Pasher, Valentine Deirs lists the following as role of the teacher in problem solving method:

(i) To give the students a chance so that they define the problem clearly.

(ii) Help the students to keep the problem in mind.

(iii) Encourage the students to come forward with their suggestions. For this he should encourage them:

(a) to analyse the situations in parts;

(b) to recall previously known similar cases and general rules that apply;

(c) to guess and formulate guesses correctly.

(iv) Allow them time to evaluate the suggestions by encouraging them.

(a) to maintain a state of doubt a suspended conclusion;

(b) to criticise the suggestion by appeal to know facts, minister experiments and scientific treatises.

(v) Get them to organise material by proceeding

(a) to build an outline on the board;

(b) to use diagrams and graphs;

(c) to formulate concise statement of the net outcome of the discussion.

11. Deductive-Inductive Methods

It is a combination of two methods. To be able to understand this combination it is necessary to understand them separately.

I. Inductive Method

In this method one is led from concrete to abstract, particular to general and from complex to general rule. In this method we prove a universal law by showing that if it is true in a particular case it is also true in other similar cases.

Merits of the Inductive Method

(i) It helps understanding.

(ii) It is a scientific method.

(iii) It develops scientific attitude.

(iv) It is a logical method and develops critical thinking and habit of keen observations.

(v) It is a psychological method and provides ample scope for students activities.

(vi) It is based on actual observations, thinking and experimentation.

(vii) It keeps alive the students interest because they move from known to unknown.

(viii) It curbs the tendency to learn by rote and also reduces home work.

(ix) It develops self-confidence.

(x) It develops the habit of intelligent hard work.

Drawbacks of Inductive Method

This method suffers from the following limitations:

(i) It is limited in range and cannot be used in solving and understanding all the topics in civics.

(ii) The generalization obtained from a few observations are not the complete study of the topic. To fix the topic in the mind of the learner a lot of supplementary work and practice is needed.

(iii) Inductive reasoning is not absolutely conclusive. The generalization has been done from the study of a few (three or four) cases. The process thus establishes certain degree of probability which can be increased by increasing the number of valid cases.

(iv) This method needs a lot of time and energy and thus it is time consuming and laborious method.

(v) This method is not found to be suitable in higher classes because some of the unnecessary details and explanations may make teaching dull and baring.

Application of Inductive Method

Its application has to be restricted and confined to understanding of rules in the early stages. This method is quite useful in lower classes where certain simple generalisation are to be made. At the advanced stage it is not so useful. This method is psychological and gives very good results if followed by *deductive method*.

II. Deductive Method

Deductive method is the opposite of the inductive method. It is based on deduction. In this method proceed from general to particular and from abstract to concrete. In this method, the rules are given at the very outset. The students are asked to apply these rules to solve more problems. In this method the formula is accepted by the students as pre-established and well-established truth which can be used by the students to solve problems.

Merits of Deductive Method

(i) It is a short and time saving method.

(ii) This method suits all types of students.

(iii) This method is suitable for all topics.

(iv) This method provides sufficient practice in the application of various mathematical formulae and rules.

(v) The speed and efficiency increases by use of this method.

(vi) It completes the process of induction. Probability in induction gets converted into certainty by this method.

Limitations

(i) It is not a scientific method because the approach of this method is confirmatory and not explanatory.

(ii) It encourages rote memory because pure deductive work requires some law; principle formula for every type of problem and it demands blind memorisation of large number of such laws/formulae etc.

(iii) Being an unscientific method it does not impart any training in scientific method.

(iv) It causes unnecessary and heavy burden on the brain which may sometimes result in brain fag.

(v) It this method memory becomes more important than understanding and intelligence which is educationally not sound.

(vi) It is an unpsychological method because the facts and principles are not found by the students themselves.

(vii) In this method students cannot become active learners.

(viii) It is not suitable for development of thinking, reasoning and discovery.

Place of Deductive Method

It is a method of work and practice. While applying deduction, great care should be exercised so that no wrong creeps in. This method works well with average students and teachers. This method provides skill, speed and efficiency in solving problem. Most teachers follow this method and even text-books are written according to this method. However, this method gives good results if it is preceded by inductive method.

Thus, we find that *induction* and deduction are complementary so beginning should be made with the inductive method which should then be followed by a sufficient *drill work* by deductive method. This promotes speed, accuracy and command of the subject. So understand mathematics inductively and apply deductively. Best results are given by Induction-deduction combination.

Conclusion

A careful consideration of merits and limitations of these two methods leads in to conclude that Inductive Method is the fore-runner of Deductive Method. For effective teaching of science, both inductive and deductive approaches should be used because no one is complete without the other. Induction leaves the learner at a point where he cannot stop and the after work has to be done and completed by deduction. Deduction is a process that is particularly suitable for final statement and induction is most suitable for exploration fields. Induction gives the lead and deduction follows.

12. Source Method

Source method implies the use of original material and original sources in the teaching of political science and civics. Source can be classified as under:

(i) Primary source.

(ii) Secondary source.

Primary Source

They include physical remains or relics of unconscious testimony in far off historical sites, roads, pyramids, human remains, clothing, food, fortification, utensils, pottery, building, implements, machinery, furniture, weapons, fine arts and museum pieces, inscriptions etc.

They also include consciously transmitted information in the form of oral or written testimony. Such written sources are constitutions, charters, court decisions, official minutes or records, autobiographies, letters, diaries, genealogies, contracts, deeds, wills, permits, licences, affidavits, depositions, declarations, proclamations, certificates, bills, receipts, magazines and newspapers, accounts, advertisements, maps, diagrams, books pamphlets, films etc.

Secondary Source

These are the sources which are written by those who are not actually on the sense of the events. e.g. An act passed by the Parliament is a primary source but its extract published in a secondary source.

Use of Source Method

It can be used at following stages of the lesson:

(1) *Pre-lesson use of resources.* Visits to actual sites of monuments,

forts or museums may be arranged. The teacher can ask the students to read selected passages connected with the lesson before hand.

(2) *Mid-lesson use of resources.* Extracts from original or secondary sources can be read during the course of the lesson. They create real situations, import reality and vividness to the lesson and reinforce the impact of teaching.

(3) *Post-lesson use of resources.* Pre-lesson use of resources can also become the post-lesson use of resources and *vice-versa.* Students may be given assignments which need the use of resources and *vice-versa.* Students may be given assignments which need the use of resources. They may be encouraged to pursue their interest in a particular topic, do some critical thinking and analysis and prepare their own account.

Advantages of the Source Method

The following advantages may be derived occasionally by following the source method:

(1) It would make facts appear real, as they are gathered from sources which can be seen or studied directly. The learner acquires greater conviction in regard to the truth of happenings.

(2) The source method provides an opportunity to the pupils to learn civics and political science by 'doing'. It is activity method. The activities may take very interesting shape in the form of visits to museums, actual handling of things in the school museum, etc.

(3) The source method offers scope for groups work—there may be a workshop for building up history in regard to a particular topic with the help of sources.

(4) This method gives the pupils an insight into the process of gathering facts and it develops the historical sense in them. The sense of objectivity which is so very important to a student of civics and political science can be particularly developed through this method.

(5) This method also gives the pupils some idea about the method of historical research; however rudimentary the idea might be. As such this method may make some contribution in developing the interest of pupils in research though they may undertake it at a much later date.

(6) Though the source method may be more suitable to the pupils of higher classes, it can also be utilised with advantage by pupils of primary classes, who many, be studying political science and civics through the source method. The source method would make their study more concrete and more meaningful.

(7) It supplements classroom lesson.

(8) It develops elementary skills of collecting data sifting the relevant and organising the same.

(9) Learning becomes functional because it is gained in the real situation.

(10) It provides opportunities for useful mental exercises—right thinking and imagining, comparing and analysing drawing inferences, etc.

Steps to be Followed in Source Method

The steps, to be followed in studying a topic through the source method are as under:

(i) The unit for study, with problems and source materials through which answers are to be sought, should first be presented to the pupils. References in regard to the source material may also be given to the pupils.

(ii) If we wish to follow the workshop technique, the class should be divided into groups with assignment of specific responsibilities, i.e., each group should be given a few specific questions whose answers it may try to find out with the help of source materials.

(iii) After this the pupils should be introduced to the sources (excursions to sites, visits to museums and the student or group should seek the solution of the problems assigned to them (the group may make its own sub-division of responsibilities among its members).

(iv) One or two class periods may then be provided to the groups for editing the notes (taken while in direct contact with the sources) and for preparing written answers to the questions assigned to them.

(v) The answers may be mutually corrected by the group according to the procedure suggested before; the teacher may also go through the answers, select the best ones and keep them in a convenient place for use by the pupils.

(vi) One class period (if it can be spared) may be devoted to the discussion of some of the controversial findings arrived at by the groups, with a view to stimulate greater interest in the work.

(vii) The groups may also be encouraged to write articles for the civics wall newspaper on the basis of their findings.

Limitations of the Source Method

1. It is very difficult for the school teachers to have an easy access to original sources.
2. Utilisation or original sources is a very difficult task for the school students as they lack the requisite training.
3. The method is very complex and technical.
4. There is the difficulty of languages. Almost all the original sources are the Sanskrit, Pali, Arabic or Persian and a few in English.
5. Contemporary authors and writers have given their won prejudices, preferences and limitation with the result that it becomes very difficult to sift fact from fiction. The students are, thus, lost in the maze of conflicting view about the same event or movement.
6. Source method of teaching is very expensive.
7. Source method of teaching is time consuming.

How to Make Source Method Effective ?

The students be encouraged to study the resource books in the library. Educational tours to places of importance may be arranged. The students may be asked to write their own impressions and inferences about the places they visit. Copies of important extracts from the relevant records may be pasted on the blackboard for the use of students.

Dr. Keatings thinks that original sources can be used for creating suitable environment in the lower form. Well planned, purposive and well-directed efforts have to be made by the teacher in the use of this method. By suggesting the use of resource method we do not aim at making our students research scholars. Use of the method in selected topics is likely to make the study of political science and civics meaningful and real.

13. Recitation or Socialised Recitation Method

Adam Wesley was one of the chief exponents of this method. He wanted to introduce a method in which the whole class acquires knowledge with the co-operation of all the students. In this method of the formal character of the classroom is intended to be dismantled. The students are encouraged to acquire knowledge according to their nature interest and the co-operation of their fellow being. In this method the students are asked to sit in the classroom in a semi-circle. The teacher takes his seat alongwith the students. This method is also known as 'Socialised Discussion Method'.

Merits or Advantage

This method of teaching has certain advantages in it.

(i) It trains the students in the art of making plans and encourages them to take up work independently. The students are also asked to take part in the discussions and debates. They are encouraged to take up independent thinking.

(ii) The students are trained in organising their experience and put them down in a written form.

(iii) This method tries to discover the interest and aptitudes of the students.

(iv) This method is helpful in creating self-confidence and self-reliance in the students.

This method requires a very careful handling. Teacher shall have to be trained before this method can be put to practice. That training programme is yet to be achieved.

14. Survey Method

In this method, the students are encouraged to discover and survey things and there by acquire knowledge. In this, the students are encouraged to survey the local conditions and environments. This method is useful for lower classes. Here the whole class is divided into various groups and each group is asked to survey a particular aspect of a subject. For example, a class may be divided into five groups—one group may be asked to survey the geographical conditions of the city, another group may be asked to survey the history of the origin and the development of the city. The third group may be asked to collect the data about to the number of shops in the city, the fourth group may be asked to collect information about occupations and local administration and other social problems.

When the students have made a survey of the fields allowed to them, they collect together and discuss them and arrive at a certain conclusion. Then they write out the conclusions in systematic manner. Maps and graphs are also drawn. These maps and charts are used for decorading the walls of the classroom.

In fact, this method of teaching is nothing but a combination of various methods. It has the element of a scientific procedure of study.

15. Dramatic Method or Dramatic Method

This method is based on the theory of 'Play'. Attempt is made to get the subject-matter enacted or dramatised with the help of the students. The students take interest in dramatising the subject-matter. While dramatising, they acquire knowledge.

This is a psychological method. The students remain active in the acquisition of knowledge.

In this method of teaching the working of the Parliament or Zila Parishads may be dramatised with the help of the students.

This method is also likely to develop the creative efforts of the educands.

Merits of the Dramatic Method

It has the following merits in it:

(1) It brings about a development of the mental faculties of the students.

(2) Through this method, interest is created in the students about the subject that has to be taught.

(3) Through this method the subject-matter of Civics is made interesting and intelligible.

(4) This method creates in the students, a sense of self-confidence and self-importance. Shyness of the students is dismantled.

(5) It also leads to development of social and moral qualities in the students. They try to liveup to the ideals of the great men whose role they play.

Requirements

This method requires certain things from the teacher:

(1) The teacher should be well-aware of the techniques of drama. He should also know the art of writing dialogues.

(2) He should have the capacity to select the dramatic material.

(3) He should also be acquainted with the qualities of simplicity and authenticity that are the requisites of dramatic procedure.

(4) The teacher should have the capacity to mould his personality accordingly as and when required. In short, he should have all that practical knowledge that is required for an efficient Drama Director.

16. Comparative Method

This method was propounded by the famous educationist, Aristolte. He was of the view the Civics is a subject which is a combination of many subjects. These subjects are similar as well as different. The teacher should, therefore, try to teach the subject of Civics on the basis of various methods. He should try to compare various things and thus impart knowledge of the Civics to the students. While resorting to comparative method, following things should be borne in mind:

(1) Conclusion should be arrived at only after comparing various things. It is not wise to compare two things only and then jump down to a conclusion.

(2) Comparison should always be done with the similar things. If the comparison is to be made of certain associations, various social, cultural, political and other associations should be taken up and they should be compared from various angles.

17. Narration Method or Method of Narration or Story Method

In this method, the teacher narrates the subject-matter before the students. He tries to explain the indirect knowledge through his direct narration. An attempt is made to present the difficult subject-matter in a simple, intelligible and interesting manner. If this method is combined by question-answer method, it becomes all the more interesting. But it is not possible to employ this method in the teaching of each and every subject. The teacher should handle this method cautiously. He should not dominate the whole scene. He should also encourage the students to remain active.

This method may be quite useful in the teaching of Civics. Certain topics may be taught in a narrative method. The teacher should keep the following things in view:

(1) In narration, the age, interest and the aptitude of the child should be borne in mind. The narrarion should be clear, systematic, interesting and well-organised. There should be perfect chronological order.

(2) The narration should have the element of administration in it. The teacher should show certain pictures etc. to the students.

(3) The voice of the teacher should be quite attractive. He should have the capacity to change his voice according to emotions and circumstances. His pronunciation should be very clear and scientific.

The following statement of Binings in regard to the method of teaching is quite important:

> "If the teaching is to reach its highest degree of efficiency, teacher must posses a broad understanding of all faces of method as a part of that Philosophy of Education which is essential to good teaching."
>
> *Bining and Bining*

Revision Questions

1. What are the various methods of teaching civic ? Which method is useful for which stage of education ?
2. Describe Text-book method of teaching of civics.
3. What are the merits and demerits of lecture method ?
4. What is a problem method ? What is the role of teacher in the problem method ?
5. Discuss inductive-deductive method.

Chapter 6

Teaching Aids in Civics

6.1 INTRODUCTION

Teaching aids should be used to supplement the process of teaching. Most of the teaching aids are sensory aids and their function is to make teaching concrete, effective and interesting. Teaching aids are the means of modernisation of methods of teaching in schools. In the absence of teaching aids lesson becomes dry and ineffective.

6.2 IMPORTANCE OF TEACHING AIDS

At present the education in child centred and no more subject-centred. Thus it is the aptitude, interest and mental powers of the children that determine the education. The aim of education is to develop and train the mental powers of the child. Teaching aids are used to make the teaching interesting.

If the education fails to create activity in the children or to awaken their interest in the subject-matter it is useless. For awakening interest the education should be practical and good.

We should make an effort to make the knowledge stable and strengthen the experiences. The method used for imparting education must be simple, interesting and intelligible . For this teacher has to make use of different methods, these methods must be such as to conform to the mental and psychological requirements of the child.

Teaching aids are the various things that bring about a better method and system of education. They add to the effectiveness and attractiveness of the teaching.

About teaching aids Bining and Bining has said:

> "Visual devices of many kinds may serve in making the abstract concrete and in arousing interest in students that would otherwise be unreal and dull."

6.3. NEED OF TEACHING AIDS

(i) These aids help the teacher getting the attention of his students.

(ii) These aids help in creating the interest of the student in the topic and activate the mental process of the students.

(iii) The student gets an opportunity to get a first hand experience by visualising some concrete things, living specimens and actual demonstrations etc.

(iv) Use of teaching aids help to have a clear conception of ideas, information, facts and principles.

(v) It helps the students in understanding some complicated and difficult concepts.

(vi) They provide an opportunity for a change in the monotonous atmosphere that generally prevails in a classroom.

(vii) They provide an opportunity for a better support between the teacher and his pupil.

(viii) They help the students to develop a scientific attitude.

(ix) They provide a training in scientific method.

(x) They can be used in bigger classes.

(xi) Use of such aids is based on the principles of psychology.

6.4 PRINCIPLES FOR USE OF TEACHING AIDS

Teaching aids should be used properly to make teaching more effective. Teaching can become more effective if such aids are used widely but the use of such aids cannot provide a guarantee of good teaching. Following points are important for use of teaching aids:

(i) Teaching aids should be woven with classroom teaching and these aids should be used only to supplement the oral and written being done in the class.

(ii) While making use of any teaching aid an effort be made that the teaching aids being used in any class are in conformity with the intellectual level of the students and is in accordance with the pervious experience of the students.

(iii) Only such aids the preferred which provide a stimulus to the students for grater thinking and activity.

(iv) If possible actual specimens be preferred to a photograph or a slide of a specimen.

(v) The teaching aid used should be exact, accurate and real as far as practicable.

(vi) The Teacher should use a teaching aid only when he is quite sure about handling a specific teaching aid. For handling some aids (e.g., operation a projector etc.) training is provided by various authorities. For this purpose more information can be obtained from local SCERT or directly from NCERT, New Delhi.

(vii) Teaching aids used be such as are closely related to pupils experiences.

(viii) The teacher should use a teaching aid only after a proper planning so that the aid is used exactly at the point; in the process of teaching, where it best fits in the process of teaching.

(ix) Teacher should see that a follow up programme follows the lesson wherein a teaching aid has been used.

(x) Teacher should carry out occasional evaluation about the use, function and effect of a teaching aid on the learning process.

6.5 TYPES OF TEACHING AIDS

For convenience of discussion the teaching aids in civics may be grouped as under :

(i) Aids used in elementary schools.

(ii) Aids used in secondary schools.

As a matter of fact no clear cut demarcation is possible but this categorisation is done only for convenience of study. The aids used in elementary schools may be called *elementary aids* and those more commonly used in secondary schools are referred to *aids useful for secondary schools.*

Materials used in the teaching of civics are of the following kinds:

(i) *Traditional aids.* These included test-books, black-boards etc.

(ii) *Visual aids.* Objects, models, pictures, charts, skretch, map etc.

(iii) *Audio-visual aids.* Radio, film strip, tape-recorder, slide projector, television etc.

6.6 MATERIAL AIDS IN TEACHING OF CIVICS AT THE PRIMARY STAGE OF EDUCATION

At this stage of education, children between 6 to 11 years of age receive education. Their social, moral, mental and physical education does not take place simultaneously and at the same speed. It differs from child to child. As the children grow, their physical and mental organs find development. Therefore, it is not possible to employ one set of teaching aids on all the students simultaneously. It should differ from stage to stage.

Primary education is the stage of early childhood of the students. Students are very fond of listening to stories. Curiosity is their predominant instinct. The teacher should make an effort to impart education by playing upon this instinct of the children. Education should be of a concrete nature.

An attempt also should be made to make the teaching interesting and attractive. Different types of teaching aids should be used but the consideration of the mental and the physical age group of the children should also be help in mind.

Text-books. At this stage children should not be taught with the help of text-books. However, the text-books may be used only for helping the students to revise and strengthen the experiences given to them in the classroom. The text-books that are used should be well-illustrated, attractive and nicely printed.

Models. At this stage of education generally Panchayats, Zila Parishads etc., are taught. Models of these things may be presented before the students. These models should be attractive and artistic. Students should been couraged to prepare such models. This shall encourage their learning by doing.

Pictures and Charts. Pictures should be freely used at this stage of education. Showing of pictures satisfaction the curiosity of the students. But while using these pictures, it should be borne in mind that they should be accurate, artistic and attractive.

Charts can also be used. These charts should be neatly drawn.

Black-board. At this stage of education black-board plays an important role, specially in teaching of Civics. Various things should be put down on the black-board, and then illustrated orally. Charts may be drawn on these boards.

An attempt should also be made to write out things legibly and it is only on the black-boards. Maps and charts should also be neatly drawn.

Home Task. Home task is not advisable at this stage of education.

6.7 MATERIAL AIDS IN THE TEACHING OF CIVICS AT THE JUNIOR HIGH SCHOOL STAGE OF EDUCATION

At this stage of education children between the age group of 11-14 are taught. This may be called the boyhood. Next stage to this is adolescence. At this stage we find children who have thinking, reasoning and such other mental faculties developed. An attempt should be made to make the teaching more realistic at this stage of education. This should be well-reflected in the use of teaching aids.

Text-books. Text-books are the traditional aids and they should be used at this stage of education.

Charts and Pictures. Picture do not have great value as an aid at this stage of education, but charts do have a value. An attempt should be made to encourage the students to draw charts.

Models. Models are useful at this stage of education. An attempt should be made to encourage the students to construct models.

Audio-visual Aids. Such aids like radio, tape recorder, film etc., may also be employed at this stage of education.

Black-board. Black-board should be properly used at this stage.

Graphs and maps etc., may be drawn on the board and the students should be asked to fill in things on the maps and graphs.

Bulletin Board. It may be used for pasting pictures and cartoons etc. This will be useful for the teaching of Civics.

6.8 MATERIAL AIDS IN THE TEACHING OF CIVICS AT THE SECONDARY STAGE OF EDUCATION

At this stage of education we have to teach the students who have a good deal of physical, moral and mental development. Students at this stage have reached or entered adolescence. They do not very much need the teaching aids. Things may be given to them in a realistic manner. However, it cannot be denied that teaching aids should be discarded at this stage of education. Teaching aids must be employed, but with a bit of realistic touch.

Text-books. Text-books should be utilised at this stage of education. The students must be asked to use the text-books in doing home task.

Black-board. Black-board should be utilised for putting down the substance of the topic taught in the class. It may also be utilised for presenting facts before the students.

Audio-visual Aids

Various audio-visual aids may be used for imparting education in a successful manner at this stage of education. Some of the audio-visual aids are given below :

(1) Television. The role of television in the present day world is becoming more and more important and it is one of the most important teaching aids. It combines the advantages of a radio (broad cast) and of a film. This can be used for mass education and now U.G.C. programmes are a regular feature on "Door Darshan". The topics of discussion are announced in advance and lesson from well-qualified persons and specialists in their fields are shown on TV. Teacher can easily plan his work accordingly and in this way he can make use of TV as a teaching aid.

(2) Radio. Television is out of question in poor country like India, but radio can be utilised. Various programmes should be organised for teaching of certain topics of Civics through radio. Certain dramas and stories may be broadcast by radio that may give to the students the knowledge of certain topics of Civics.

Radio can also serve as an effective aids in teaching of Civics.

Such lessons may be planned which may be broadcast from the radio and they may provided a back ground to the knowledge of civics. Special programmes may be designed for students which have a bearing on the subject-matter of civics. It is also possible to listen to the description of towns and other things on radio. Broadcast talks are now a regular feature of All India Radio.

All India Radio has in its regular feature some programmes meant for school children. In such a programme generally talks on educational matters are broadcast teacher. Such a talk is quite useful for students as also for civics teacher.The topic, date and time of broadcast of such are given in advance by All India Radio.

(3) Film Projectors and Cinemas. At this stage of education students grow interest in films. This agency may be employed for imparting education of Civics to the students. Films depicting various events of civic importance. Such as elections, may be depicted through films. Working of a democracy may also be shown through films.

Film projectors are the means of showing films. With the help of this instrument a film may be projected right into the classroom.

These are further improvements on the teaching aids discussed so far. These have brought about a revolution in teaching of geography. Geography films are shown to the students to illustrate various topics as also to supplement the classroom teaching. Both type of films have some basic ojectives to serve.

Film Strip-projector

It is an improvement on magic lantern and this machine can be used to project many a topics on a single strip. One such strip generally consists of 40-100 separate pictures and such film strips are available on loan from Central Film Library, NCERT, New Delhi. On such a film strip pictures concerning one topic are arranged in a definite order.

This machine can be easily handled by the teacher. The machine is operated by hand and thus can be stopped at the discretion of the teacher whenever, he wants to explain some aspect of a topic being shown on machine.

Micro-projector

This projector is generally operated in a dark room. The projection can be taken on vertical screen whole class is expected to see it. However, such a film cannot be distinctly seen by a student if he is sitting at a distance more than 12 feet from the screen.

Film Projector

This machine is used for showing geography films. Some good science films on various topics are available and these can be had on loan sometimes even free of charge from the source.

Precautions. The teacher should take the following precautions whenever he wants to use a film projection as a teaching aid :

(i) He should satisfy himself about the lighting management and seating arrangement in the room where such film show is to be given.

(ii) He should himself see the film before hand.

(iii) He should give a complete background of the film to the students before the actual screening of the film.

(iv) He should see that complete calm and peace is maintained during the screening of the film.

(v) Immediately after the film show, he should invite comments, questions etc., from the students and try to answer all the quarries of the students.

(vi) He should encourage some of his students to write articles etc., based on the film show and such articles etc., may be shown on wall magazine, may be printed in school magazine.

(4) Tape Recorders and Film Strips. Through tape recorders, speeches of important leaders may be reproduced before the students, may be in the classroom, and through film strips subjects may be made more clear.

6.9 MAIN ADVANTAGES OF THE AUDIO-VISUAL AIDS

(i) Best motivators.

(ii) Fundamental to verbal instructions.

(iii) Clear images.

(iv) Vicarious experience.

(v) Variety.

(vi) Freedom.

(vii) Opportunity to handle and manipulate.

6.10 PROBLEMS IN THE USE OF TEACHING AIDS

Though these aids are becoming more and more popular every day yet there are certain problems that are faced and must be solved. These are :

(i) *Apathy of the Teachers*

Teachers are not yet convinced that teaching with words alone is quite tedious, wasteful and ineffective.

(ii) *Indifference of Students*

The judicious use of aids arouses interest but if used without a definite purpose they lose their significance and importance.

(iii) *Ineffectiveness of the Aids*

Because of the absence of proper planning and the lethargy of the teacher and without proper preparation, correct presentation, appropriate application and discussion and the essential follow up work, the aids have not proved their full usefulness. A film like a good lesson has various steps—preparation, presentation, application and discussion.

(vi) *Financial Hurdles*

The central and state governments have set up Boards of Audio-visual Education and have chalked out interesting programmes for the popularisation of teaching aids but the lack of finances is not enable them to do their best.

(v) *Absence of Electricity*

Most of the projectors cannot work in the absence of electricity which is not readily available these days.

(vi) *Lack of Facilities for Training*

At present we do not have sufficient number of training institutes and more and more teaching colleges or specialised agencies should be opened to train teachers and workers in the use and usefulness of these aids.

(vii) *Co-ordination between Centre and States*

Good film libraries, museum of audio-visual education, fixed and mobile exhibitions and educational 'melas' should be organised both by centre and the states.

(viii) *Language Difficulty*

Most films are in English. We should have them in Hindi and other Indian languages.

(ix) *Not Catering to Local Needs*

No attention is paid in the production of Audio-visual aids to the sociological, psychological and pedagogical factors.

(x) *Improper Selection of Films*

Films are not selected according to the Classroom needs.

6.11 FUTURE OF TEACHING AIDS

Today, the problem is not whether visual aids should have a place in education. This has been recognised long ago. The problem, now, is that of extending the benefits of the teaching aids to all the teachers and students. The future of these aids can be bright if we make a proper planning and carry out good co-ordination between producers, teachers and students useful and effective aids can be produced only after getting the reaction of the audience and by carrying out a good deal of research work in the field.

Revision Questions

1. What kinds of material aids would you suggest in the teaching of Civics to inculcate civics ideals among the students and why ?

2. Define audio-visual aids and give the main reasons for their use.
3. Give a brief account of the audio-visual aids in the teaching of Civics.
4. Discuss the importance of the following in the teaching of Civics:
   (a) Chart
   (b) Motion pictures
   (c) Diagrams, and
   (d) Pictures.

Chapter 7

Techniques of Teaching Civics

7.1 INTRODUCTION

Truly speaking techniques do not have their individual capacity. They are the part and parcel of teaching methods. They are just like the ways of teaching civics to students at different stages of education. They are an additional help to the methods of teaching. They are used to make teaching more effective and more interesting.

According to **Prof. M.P. Moffat**. "All techniques should be in live with the democratic process and relate to the goals desired in the study of the topic. Techniques are employed for getting the learning under way with guidance from the teacher. They should be selected as a means of serving the best purpose of a particular line with the resultant growth for the individual."

There are many a techniques that could be effectively used for the teaching of civics. Some of these are :

(i) Drill technique

(ii) Question-answer technique

(iii) Exposition technique

(iv) Assignment technique

(v) Supervised study technique

(vi) Dramatisation

(vii) Panel discussion.

7.2 VARIOUS TECHNIQUES OF TEACHING CIVICS

1. Question-Answer Technique

Question have a very important place in the teaching of civics. By questioning the students may be kept active and alive. The teacher can also test if he has succeeded in imparting the knowledge of the subject taught. We can call it as the examination while teaching. Thus technique has special significance in the present system of education.

Significance of Questioning

Ryburn has rightly observed, "It is no exaggeration to say that the success of a teacher in any particular lesson, are in teaching in general, depends upon his ability of question well."

According to Raymont, "The acquisition of a good style of questioning may be laid down definitely as one of the essential ambitions of young teacher."

Recognising the importance of question Colvin observes, "The efficiency of instructions is measured in a large degree by the nature of the questions that are asked and the care with which they are framed. No teacher of elementary ar secondary school subjects can succeed in his instructions who has not a fair mastery of the act of questioning."

One who questions faultlessly teaches effectively, is not without meaning. Salmon holds that a bad questioner is a bad teacher, he may be a good teacher.

Purpose of Questioning

Question are generally asked :

(i) To test the previous knowledge of the students.

(ii) To enable the students to recall something.

(iii) To enable the students to recognise something.

(iv) To enable the students to think over something.

(v) To enable the students to reason about something.

(vi) To elicit some piece of information from students.

(vii) To keep the students mentally alert and attentive.

(viii) To promote initiative and originality in students.

(ix) To arouse the curiosity of the students.

(x) To find out if the students are following the lesson or not.

(xi) To link new knowledge with the previous knowledge of the students.

(xii) To revise the lesson.

(xiii) To get the co-operation of the students.

(xiv) To formulate some general rules.

Classification of the Questions

Questions may be of various types. Following are the various types of questions :

(a) Questions that awaken and develop memory.

(b) Reasoning questions.

(c) Organising questions.

(d) Informative questions.

(e) Evaluating questions.

(f) Comparative questions.

(g) Analytic questions.

(h) Thought-provoking questions.

(i) Interpretative questions.

(j) Judicative questions.

Questions based on the process of teaching. The process of teaching passes through certain stages. First of all, we introduce the topic and then we develop it, and try to test the knowledge acquired by the students. This process is achieved by recapitulation. Questions are based on this topic as well. They are of the following types.

(a) Introductory questions.

(b) Developing questions.

(c) Testing and recapitulatory questions.

Other Classification of Questions

Questions are classified on the basis of certain other things as well. They are intended to bring out the details or present the details. Thus, we can classify them as under :

(a) Detailed questions.

(b) Topical questions.

(c) Problematic questions.

Types of Questions

Questions are generally of the following types :

(i) Recall

(ii) Comparison.

(iii) Contrast.

(iv) Evaluation.

(v) Cause.

(vi) Effect

(vii) Illustration

(viii) Classification

(ix) Generalisation

(x) Definition

(xi) Proof

(xii) Description

(xiii) Characterisation

(xiv) Relationship

(xv) Summary.

Techniques of Questioning

Following points be given due consideration in this regards :

(i) The question should be asked first and then the student be asked to answer it .

(ii) Questions should be evenly distributed. No child should be neglected.

(iii) Sufficient time be given to the student to think out an answer to the question asked.

(iv) The teacher should accept the inability of a student to answer a question and should not waste much time to elicit an answer out of a student.

(v) Teacher must not ask a number of questions in a rapid fire manner otherwise the students will be upset.

Qualities of Good Questions

Questions that are put to the students should be scientifically planned. They should be good and pointed. Some of the qualities of good questions are as follows :

(i) Short and pointed

(ii) The *Language* of a question should be *simple.*

(iii) *Language* of a question should be *easy* and *intelligible.*

(iv) Questions should be *very clear.*

(v) Questions should be *graded.*

(vi) Questions should be suited to the ability of the children to whom they are put.

(vii) Questions should be relevant to the topic.

(viii) Normally the questions should not be repeated.

(ix) Teacher should try to vary the form of his questions.

(x) Questions should be of developing nature.

(xi) Suggestive questions should be avoided.

(xii) Leading questions should not be asked.

(xiii) Echo questions should not be asked.

(xiv) Questions should be no framed that they help the student in awakening his thinking power.

(xv) All the questions should be connected with one central point.

Art of Questioning

There is nothing particular about this art. Questions should be so put that they meet all the requirements of good questions. The teacher should know the qualities that a good question should possess and should put the questions in that very manner.

The Teachers Attitude to Pupil's Questions

A good teacher should have a sympathetic and encouraging attitude to the pupil's questions. For this he should

(i) encourage the students to ask questions;

(ii) insist an relevancy in questions ;

(iii) insist on courtesy;

(iv) not allow a number of students to ask the questions simultaneously;

(v) be frank enough to admit his inability to answer a question when he does not know the answer. For the sake of prestige in the eyes of the students, he should not give a wrong answer.

Judicious Blending of Talking and Questioning

Since questioning is not a one way traffic so in this process it is essential that both teacher and students actively participate in it.

Skill in Answering

The quality and the nature of answers reveals whether the purpose of questioning are fulfilled or not. Questioning is a means to teach something that is revealed through the answers. Both questions and answers are indispensable in teaching-learning process.

Answers reveal the deficiency of the students as well as teachers. They are the touchstone to the teaching—learning process. Answers are an important tool to make necessary changes in Teaching-learning process.

Classification of Answers

The answers can be placed under one of the following categories :

(i) *Right and Correct answer*

(ii) *Correct but incomplete answer*

(iii) *Partially correct and partially wrong answer*

(iv) *Wrong but intelligent answer*

(v) *Ridiculously wrong answer*

(vi) *Mischievous answer.*

There are no general or specified rules to deal with an answer. However, following are the general ways to deal with answers.

(i) *Appreciation.* Not only good and correct answers be appreciated but teacher should appreciate even wrong answers in case he feels that the child is making a genuine attempt to give an answer. The appreciations will encourage the students to think further.

(ii) *Analysis of Wrong Answer.* If the answers given by most of the students are wrong, the teacher should analyse the causes. The causes may be as under :

(a) Difficult or defective language of the question

(b) Defective explanations of the subject-matter taught.

(c) In attentiveness on the part of students.

(d) Lapse of Memory.

(e) Toughness and complexity of the subject-matter.

(iii) *Encouragement of the children.*

(iv) *Treatment of wrong answer.*

(v) *Answers carrying some other version than the one expected by the teacher.*

In such a case the teacher should explain to the students the difference in approach.

(vi) *Form of the answers according to the nature of the lesson.*

(vii) *Answers based on right understanding.*

(viii) *Answers given in unison.* Such answers should be discouraged.

(ix) *Observance of courtesy.*

(x) *Encouragement to shy and submissive students.*

(xi) *Repetition of good answers.*

(xii) *Discouragement of irrelevant answers.*

(xiii) *Development of summary of the lesson with the help of the answers.*

Right and correct answers imply that the teacher is using right and correct methods of teaching and the students are learning in an appropriate answer. It can thus be concluded that the pupil's answers to the questions are equally important if not more than questions of the teacher in teaching-learning process.

2. Assignment Technique

Assignment is a work allotment. It is the work assigned to the student. It may be done by the student at home or at school. There may be a pre-lesson or post-lesson assignment. Assignment is a sort of undertaking or commitment on the part of the learner. He undertakes upon himself the responsibility of carrying out the work assigned. It may consist of solving a few mathematical problems, understanding a proposition, solving riders based on proposition, making many propositions of the same type, preparing illustrations for a topic, collecting mathematical data, finding out applications of mathematical knowledge, tracing out historical background of a mathematical concept. Formulating problem on a topic, carrying out a mathematical project and so on.

Assignment is a sort of self-study which supplements classroom teaching. In this technique, the teacher assign work, provides guidelines and sets time limit for the completion of assignment. The teacher may write it on the black-board, dictate it or it may be given in the form of a cyclostyled or typed sheet.

Various Steps in the Assignment

In the assignment of work the following steps are involved :

(i) *Planning of the assignment work.* The teacher has to select work according to the level of the pupils and the time available.

(ii) *Providing guidelines.* Assignment is actually a directed study, merely dictating of questions or problems is not an assignment. Hints have to be given for the successful completion of assign ment.

(iii) *Supervising the work assigned.* The work of the students should be supervised if it is to be done in the classroom.

(iv) *Evaluating the assignment work.* The assignment work be carefully checked and mistakes point out.

Characteristics of Assignment

The importance characteristics of assignment are as under :

(i) It should have correlation with previous knowledge and experiences of the pupil.

(ii) It should have clarity and definiteness.

(iii) It should help in removal of pupils difficulties.

(iv) It should be stimulating.

(v) It should take into consideration the individual differences.

Suggestions for Effective Assignment

(i) The purpose of assignment should be clear to the teacher as well as to the students.

(ii) The assignment should be properly planned, keeping in mind the level of students and the availability of time.

(iii) Assignment must have clear-cut hints. So that the pupils can do the work following these directions.

(iv) Assignment should be directed at the weak points of students. It should clarity their doubts or misunderstanding.

(v) The assignments should be given according to the individual differences in pupils. The bright and weak pupils should not be given same type of assignment.

(vi) The teacher must put in hard work to devise suitable assignments and familiarise himself with the teaching-learning material relevant to the assignment.

(vii) The assignment work should be a cooperative activity wherein the teacher and the pupils participate actively.

(viii) The assignment work should be properly checked and mistakes be pointed out.

The assignment if properly planned and evaluated, cultivates the habit of self-study in the pupils. Pupils learn to finish the work with their own efforts. It is a sort of self-study which supplements class teaching. The success or effectiveness of assignment depends on the amount of work done independently by the students.

3. Home Assignment

It cannot be expected that all learning could be done during school time. School time is not sufficient to exhaust everything meant to be taught during the course of the year. Since in Mathematics a lot of practice is needed in the application of rules so home-work has to be given regularly to provide for application and practice and to supplement class-room teaching. The home-work in Mathematics may consist of some problems based on facts taught in the class. Students may be asked to learn certain principles, facts, definitions etc., by heart, they may be asked to draw graphs, charts etc.

Perhaps if the school time is used sincerely and efficiently home-work may not be necessary. Under normal conditions, the child does a good amount of work in the school. Giving home-work means creating in the child 'school feeling' at home also. Some teachers have a liking for home-work and they over burden the students with home-work. However, assigning of home work has been criticised by many an educationists. The criticism is based on the following grounds :

(i) It may adversely affect the health of the students.

(ii) It is educationally unsound to load the child with home-work.

(iii) It deprives the children of their leisure time.

(iv) A large amount of home work may create a distaste for school in the child.

(v) In quite a few homes, the conditions may not be congenial for the child to do the home-work.

(vi) The constant anxiety of doing home-work may adversely affect the progress of studies.

(vii) Sometimes it may lead to a disgraceful reaction towards the subject which may be transferred onwards to the teacher.

Utility of Home-Assignment

The importance and need of home-work cannot be minimised. The advantages of home-work may be summarised as under :

(i) It supplements class teaching.

(ii) It develops a habit of independent work in the students.

(iii) It develops a habit of regularity in the students.

(iv) It makes a proper utilisation of the leisure time of the students, which otherwise would have been wasted.

(v) It is a practical means to cover comfortably the lengthly and heavy syllabi.

(vi) It serves as a link for parent-teacher co-operation.

Suggestions for Making Home-Assignment More Useful

Home-work can become more useful if following suggestions are kept in mind while assignment home-work:

(i) Home work should be well-graded.

(ii) Its nature and amount must be determined by the individual's capacity and interest and not by the whims of the teacher.

(iii) It should neither be too easy or too difficult.

(iv) It should not be assigned as a sort of punishment.

(v) Home-work should be based on the principle taught in the class.

(vi) While assigning home-work, home conditions of the individual children be kept in mind.

(vii) Home-work time table should be prepared in advance in consultation with other subject teachers.

(viii) Home-work should be regularly corrected and checked. If the home-work is not checked, the students may fall into the bad habit of evading it or copying it.

(ix) Home-work may be of practical type. Making a model collecting some data or solving a riddle etc.

(x) It should be assessed as a part of the overall assessment of a student.

(xi) Home-work should appear enjoyable, useful and attractive. It should suit the individual speed and interests.

(xii) It should be intelligently planned and selectively assigned.

Correction of Home-Assignment

In Mathematics teaching checking of home-work is must, otherwise many mistakes or faulty processes may become fixed in the minds of students. However, regular correction of home work is also very difficult as the time-table period may be wholly consumed by the teacher for the purpose. To overcome this the teacher may divide the students into groups and brilliant students may be appointed group leaders for the purpose. Their help may be sought as and when required. The teacher may have some sample checking everyday and thorough checking occasionally. The teacher can also introduce cross checking or checking by mutual exchange of note-books. The teacher may indicate the correct solutions on the blackboard.

The problem of correction work becomes light in case the pupils have thoroughly understood the subject. If the students have not understood it, they will commit more errors. The errors will be minimum when there is thorough understanding of the subject-matter and neat systematic work that should be insisted on by the teacher.

Home-assignment is very useful, rather indispensable in Mathematics. But it should be properly planned and regular checked. Such remarks that shall encourage even those students who correct their mistakes. This would enable students to correct their mistakes and do things correctly in future.

While verifying the written work, the teacher should also have a look at the corrected work. If he does so, then students shall try to do the written work correctly.

7.3 DRILL

Drill is a way to revise a lesson that has already been taught. Thus, it is a means to strengthen the knowledge already acquired. Drill work is based on the principle of learning by doing and on the law of exercises. It is an admitted fact that practice makes a man perfect. Psychologically it has been found that learning is followed by forgetting.

Functions or Importance of Drill

Drill is an important device to fix an impression in the minds of the pupils. Making use of drill we can expect speed and accuracy in solving mathematical problems. Through drill it is possible to test the knowledge and strengthen the knowledge acquired by the students. Its importance is felt and realised in the teaching of Arithmetic. Arithmetic requires more of practice and exercise. Rewriting tables makes the knowledge perfect in lower classes.

The importance of drill can be summarised as under :

(i) It is the most effective means of fixing the impression of learned facts in mind.

(ii) It helps in development of communicational skills. Such skills are quite helpful in learning of Algebra, Arithmetic and Geometry.

(iii) It gives a sense of achievement and confidence and so it proves a positive stimulus for further learning.

(iv) It helps in developing speed and accuracy in learning of mathematics.

(v) It helps in clarifying even the minutest details of the topic.

(vi) It has been found quite useful particularly in case of average or below average students.

(vii) Drill is quite helpful in revision and review work.

(viii) Drill provides an opportunity to the student to work independently.

Advantages of the Drill

Merits of the Drill. Drill has the following merits :

(1) It keeps the teacher conscious of his responsibilities. It does not allow him to sleep over the matter for the year because he shall have to teach the students in the next class.

(2) It keeps the students awake. They have to work regularly, so as not fail in the examination.

(3) It helps the school authorities to know about the work that has been done in the class.

(4) It is helpful in strengthening the knowledge of the students. It gives an opportunity to the teacher and the authorities to award

proper position to the students in the class.

(5) Through this method, it becomes possible to distinguish between the dull and the bright students. Bright students shall be able to solve the exercises rapidly.

(6) It helps the teacher to know the weakness of the students and provide individual attention to them.

Demerits of the Drill or Exercise

In spite of the various advantages enumerated above, this method has certain drawbacks. These are as under :

(1) It provides an opportunity to the teacher to sit at ease in the class and ask the students to solves exercises or do the drill.

(2) If exercises are not properly given to the students, it is likely to jeopardise the interest of the students in subject.

(3) If not properly handled, it is possible that the students may ask some one else to help them in their work. This would make them dependent upon others. Thus the very object of teaching of Mathematics i.e., creation of the feeling of self-dependence, shall be done away with.

Importance of Drill and Exercises in the Teaching of Arithmetic

Although drill and exercises occupy an important place in the teaching of the Mathematics as a subject, yet its importance is more felt and realised in the teaching of Arithmetic. Arithmetic needs more of practice and exercise. The teachers know very well that rewriting of charts and tables makes the knowledge perfect in lower classes. The teacher of Arithmetic should try to give the exercises that are psychological and proper. He should try to give the exercises based on the subject or topic already taught. After examining the achievements of the students and correcting their mistakes he should proceed further. The teacher should try not only to encourage the students to do exercises accurately, but also try not to discourage the students who commit mistakes.

Precautions in Regard to Drills and Exercises

This method should be employed with proper care and precaution. If the following precautions are not taken, the purpose is likely to be defeated :

The following points be kept in mind to make drill work more effective and useful :

(i) Drill work should be properly planned. The teacher should be clear about the timing of drill work and the quantum of drill work needed at a particular stage.

(ii) Drill work should follow understanding. The teacher should make sure that the students have understood the facts or rules. Only then, drill work is useful. In the absence of understanding, they may repeat a number of wrong things.

(iii) It should be an interesting affair, and not become boring or unpleasant. The teacher may use teaching aids and also introduce play spirit in drill work.

(iv) It should be meaningful. The students must know why they are having drill in a particular topic and the purpose behind it.

(v) The drill work should be individualised to the maximum possible extent. All the students do not have the same level of learning and intelligence. The consideration of individual differences should always be kept in mind.

(vi) The drill work should always be based on the facts taught. New facts or rules should not be given in drill work.

(vii) The drill work should be moderate and should not be continued for a long time otherwise it is likely to create distaste and boredom.

(viii) It should be properly supervised. The students may commit certain mistakes. These should be immediately identified and corrected.

(ix) Drill work should be varied. It should not always be of the same type otherwise it will become monotonous.

(x) For success in drill, the drill work should be graded properly.

(xi) Drill work should never be given as punished. Drill assignments should not be made tasks.

(xii) The achievements of learners should be evaluated frequently.

(xiii) The teacher should provide proper environment for drill work.

Thus the effective drill requires proper planning and careful supervision. Only then it leads to perfecting skills and maintenance of good results.

7.4 SUPERVISED STUDY

By *supervised study,* we mean to study under the supervision of the teacher. The students are asked to solve problems or to do some practical work in the school hours or even in the afternoon if it is a residential school. The teacher gives guidance and direction on the spot. The study may be individual or collective. The students are free to work independently or to perform activities in consultation with their teacher. It is the responsibility of the teacher to see that the students make efforts in the right direction.

Importance of Supervised Study

Supervised study has been found to be helpful in a number of ways in the teaching of mathematics. For example:

(i) It helps in creating a suitable atmosphere for the self-study of the students.

(ii) It helps in providing on the spot help and guidance to the students.

(iii) It provides enough scope for mutual consultation amongst students as also amongst student and teacher whenever the need arises.

(iv) It helps the teacher in knowing about the doubts and difficulties of individual pupils. Such a knowledge is useful for teacher and he is then in a better position to understand and guide the students.

(v) The presence of the teacher makes the atmosphere of learning more congenial and the students have to complete the work given to them.

(vi) It is helpful in development of the habit of regularity, punctuality, and systematic work.

(vii) It helps to save time as also energy of students as they are guided in the right direction.

(viii) It helps in solving the problem of indiscipline because the students are kept busy in one or the other thing.

How to make Supervised Study More Effective ?

Following points if kept in view will help to make supervised study more effective:

(i) It should be well-planned after taking into consideration the work to be accomplished, the time that is available and they type of students etc.

(ii) For success of supervised study a congenial atmosphere, in the classroom, should be ensured.

(iii) The student be allowed sufficient freedom to work in their own way.

(iv) The teacher should provided only the minimum essential guidance.

(v) In case of large classes, the students be asked to work in small groups. For supervision work the teacher may take the help of bright students or he may ask some other teachers for such a help.

(vi) All efforts be made to see that the work of students has been individualised because all the students do not have the same speed, interest and achievement level.

(vii) Efforts be made to pay individual attention to the student.

(viii) The period of supervised study should not be too long.

(ix) The teacher should supervise the work of students actively and he should not sit passively in a corner.

Drawbacks of Supervised Study

Some of the drawbacks of supervised study are as under :

(i) It overburdens the teacher because he has to plan, supervise and guide pupils individually. Thus it demands too much work from the teacher.

(ii) In supervised study the teacher is required to supervise and guide pupils individually. Such a supervision may not be possible in large classes.

(iii) The teacher may be tempted to provide too much guidance, which amounts to interference in the free work of pupils. Guidance should be neither too much nor too little.

(iv) The supervision may become purposeless, when it is done by the teachers merely to keep the students busy or to penalise them.

(v) The teacher should not be very strict, otherwise the students will be afraid to consult him.

Supervised study is a useful technique and it trains the students to work independently. They need guidance, the need of the teacher is desirable. As the students learn to work themselves, the amount of guidance should be decreased. The success of the technique depends upon teacher's devotion and hard work. A well-organised and supervised study is quite helpful in learning Mathematics. The teacher should remember the goal of supervised study, the ultimate goal is self-learning.

7.5 SELF-STUDY

Self-study means independent work to be carried out by the students. In self-study, the individual studies and learns by himself. He attempts and solves every problem himself. So self-study is a habit of independent learning so that the students are able to solve problems acquire knowledge and skills of Mathematics with their own independent efforts.

Importance of Self-Study

(i) It prepares the students for real life where he cannot depend on others.

(ii) By self-study the students learn to make use of their knowledge in tacking various problems.

(iii) Self-study is the best way to supplement class-teaching. Self-study is the best way to practice various things.

(iv) Self-study develops problem-solving and heuristic attitude in the students. It also develops initiative and independent thinking in the students.

(v) It helps in widening the mental horizon of the students.

(vi) It discourages cramming.

(vii) It builds up self-confidence in the students and they do not hesitate in tacking problems.

(viii) It helps in proper utilisation of leisure time.

(ix) It helps in developing the interest of the students in the learning of Mathematics.

Suggestion of Encouraging Self-Study

To encounter self-study the following points are quite useful :

(i) An effort be made to convince the students about the fact that Mathematics is best learnt through self-effort.

(ii) An all out effort be made to inculcate the habit of self-study in the students at the earliest possible stage.

(iii) The teacher should adopt, Heuristic method of teaching, in the classroom. He should encourage independent work on the part of the students.

(iv) Teacher should properly grade the work that he wishes to accomplish through self-study.

(v) Teacher should encourage the students to make proper and full use of library books. For this he may suggest them certain interesting readings.

(vi) The students be also trained to take notes in independent self-study.

(vii) The teacher should ask the students to read a topic in advance, before taking it up in the class.

(viii) The students who study independently should be praised publicly.

(ix) The co-operation of parents should be sought to ensure regular progress of a student in self-study.

(x) The work accomplished by the student in self-study should be checked, corrected and evaluated by the teacher.

Self-study is the most effective technique in teaching of Mathematics. The teacher must cultivate this habit in himself. As and when possible, he should encourage this habit in the students.

7.6 GROUP DISCUSSION

There are a number of techniques which can be effectively used for the teaching of Mathematics. *Group work* is one of them.

Groups work is a via-media between class teaching and the individuals independent work, since individual methods of work are almost impossible under the present circumstances and class teaching does not fulfill the purposes of modern education. We have to strike a via media in the form of Group work. It is for these reason that we started to think of team teaching, tutorial seminars and symposium in teaching of Mathematics.

Group work aims at securing the advantages of individualized instructions retaining at the same time the economic and socially advantageous way of teaching the students together. The large and unmanageable class is divided into small and manageable groups. The groups are formed keeping in view the abilities, interest, achievements and speed of the pupils. The pupils in a group are almost of the same level. In such a smaller unit it is possible to pay individual attention. In such a group over individualism is also avoided. In such groups pupils work under groups feeling and there is more co-operation, homogeneity and healthy competition.

The Importance of group work is summarised below :

(i) Group work is useful in large classes, where there are wide individual differences. The pupils of almost the same level are put in the same group.

(ii) Group work facilities mutual exchange of views. The students are able to consult the members of the group and the teacher. It develops in them social habits such as co-operation etc.

(iii) It solves the problem of paying individual attention.

(iv) It provides healthy change in the classroom atmosphere.

(v) For doing project work, group work is very useful. Group work provides opportunities for effective learning of Mathematics.

Scope of Group Work

In Mathematics there is ample scope for group work. The students may voluntarily engaged in group work for doing their home work. They pool their resources and thus complete the assignment jointly which none of them may be capable to do single handed.

If a teacher chooses to do his teaching through activities projects, assignment or practical work, the students find opportunity for group work. Preparation of a mathematical model or some other material will require a group of students to work in co-operation. If the mathematics room is to be decorated and equipped for the subject, it will be a group work for the students.

Group work can thus be used when

(i) Home work is to be done.

(ii) Assignments are to be completed jointly.

(iii) Oral drill is conducted in the earlier stages.

(iv) Activities, practical work, project work etc. are to be completed.

(v) Mathematics room is to be decorated etc. etc.

Suggestions for Effective Use of Group Work

Following points be kept in view :

(i) As far as possible, the group should be homogenous in level of intelligence and level of achievement.

(ii) The group should neither be too large nor be too small. It should have members from 3 to 7 but there cannot be any rigidity about it.

(iii) A single student should not be encouraged to monopolise the group work. Teacher should ensure that every member of the group share the work (activity).

(iv) The purpose of group work should be adequately clear.

(v) The teacher should actively guide the work of the pupils.

(vi) The teacher should encourage healthy group competition but should guard against mutual jealousies or differences.

Limitations of Group Work

As in every other technique of teaching so also in group work there are certain limitations some of these are as under :

(i) It provides a scope to shrink work. In a group certain students simply do not work. They let others work.

(ii) Group work does not clearly indicate individual progress. It indicates the progress of the group only.

(iii) Various members of a particular group do not get all the knowledge from their own experiences. They perform only specific duties and activities, hence their knowledge may also be partial.

(iv) The working within the group sometimes lead to certain dissensions and differences. As a result the group work suffers seriously.

(v) The group work may not suit in higher classes. It may not suit all topics.

However, group work is quite useful when the teacher properly plans, organised and supervised group work. He must know when and how group work should be used.

7.7 EXPOSITION TECHNIQUE

Exposition is the process of making the difficult things easy. In this technique attempt is made to explain difficult words, portions, pieces, etc. In the teaching of the language, this technique is quite useful. This technique is useful in the teaching of social studies as well, but it is more useful in the teaching of language. In the teaching of Civics, we have to reach a particular objective. It is quite possible that the narration of those topics may have certain difficult portions. Through exposition technique those portions may be made easy and intelligible.

The teacher may employ this technique with the help of proverbs, quotations, sayings etc.

Revision Questions

1. Describe briefly the various techniques of teaching civics.
2. Give an account of various techniques of teaching civics. Also state which technique is best and why ?
3. Describe in detail how to make use of modern techniques in teaching of civics ?

Chapter 8

Text-Books and Their Importance in Teaching of Civics

8.1 INTRODUCTION

Text-books are standardized collection of the subject-matter that has to be taught to the students. They facilitate the teaching of new concepts and skills and maintain knowledge already acquired and help the correlation of the theoretical knowledge with the practical aspects of life. There are three categories of text-books :

(i) Reference books

(ii) Main text-books, and

(iii) Supplementary books.

8.2 IMPORTANCE OF TEXT-BOOKS

Before script came into existence and press came into being, most of the education was imparted orally and verbally. This tradition was all the more prevalent in India. It was at a very late stage that text-books came to be used in education. In the western world, it was after French Revolution that text-books came to be used in education. Later on in America this device was employed. Since then they are being used. In India the text-books were used after script came into existence and the verbal knowledge was transcribed on the leaves of the trees. In the Islamic world, Holy Quran formed the text-book of the earliest education of the child. This was also a written book.

Text-books have an importance in the field of education. They are a device of importing knowledge to the students. They save a lot of time and economise the human labour. H.R. Duglus has rightly said that, " In the last analysis will the great majority of the teachers, the text-book is potented detriment of what and how they will teach.

The teacher is the workman, who moulds the lives of the students into various forms. He has to use the text-books as the instruments. If the instruments are not good the workman shall not be able to present his best. Similarly, if the text-books are not good, the teacher is not able to present the best before the students. Raymont has rightly said :

> "The text-book must be regarded as strictly subordinate and supplementary to the teacher lesson."

8.3 VALUE OF GOOD TEXT-BOOK

The value of a good text-book of Mathematics is considered under various headings :

(a) Utility to the teacher.

(b) Utility to the student.

(c) Utility to maintain uniform standards.

Utility of Text-books in the Teaching of Civics

A great deal of controversy exists about the utility of text-books in the teaching of social studies. Since civics is a part of social studies so the controversy engulfs this subject as well. Some educationist have opined that text-books should not be used at all while others are of the opinion that the text-books should form the real base of education. Both these opinions are the extremes. Actually the best way is to strike a balance between the two. Text-books should be used in teaching of civics but they should be used economically. They should be used to help the students to strengthen their experiences or to help the students to revise their lessons which they have learnt in the classroom. Text-books can also be used by the students to write down the answers to the questions that the teacher asks them to write down.

Text-books should serve as tools in the hands of the teachers. They should help the teachers to make their teaching more authentic, successful and effective. Earnest Horne has rightly remarked :

> "One of the most effective ways for improving the content and method of instruction is to place better text-books in the hands of teachers and pupils."

In this regards Prof. Hardikar says, "The text-book is a totality of items of knowledge, habits, feelings, activities and attitudes."

(A) Utility to the Teacher

(i) It provides suitable subject-matter and guidelines regarding the syllabus of the subject. So the teacher neglects no portion of the syllabus and does not waste time on irrelevant details.

(ii) It helps the teacher to teach in an organised and systematic way, as it contains various topics in a proper sequence.

(iii) It is the most reliable source of information as it is generally written experienced teachers. It serves as a reference book to the teacher.

(iv) A good text-book suggests the steps of planning, method of teaching and suitable illustrative materials to the teacher, regarding a particular topic.

(v) It provides certain well-illustrated examples about a topic.

(vi) It provides the teacher with a number of well-graded problems which he can give to the students.

(vii) Text-books help the teacher in assigning home-work to his students. They also help him to assign drill work.

(viii) It also suggests possibilities of correlation and related project activities.

(B) Utility of the Students

Text-books are quite useful from the point of view of students as they save their time and they are saved from taking class notes.

Some other uses are :

(i) They provide the students with well-graded exercises for drill, revision and review.

(ii) Text-books helps a student to understand the subject-matter as it makes the things clear.

(iii) Since every text-book contains some solved problems so the student can take help of these problems in solving other unsolved problems.

(iv) The student can learn a topic in advance with the help of text-book.

(v) Text-books are also quite useful in case a student has to remain absent from class due to one or the other reason.

(C) Utility to Maintain Uniform Standards

Text-books play an important role of maintaining a uniformity in standards. The text-books are quite helpful to examiners in their evaluation work became they come to know of the standards expected of a particular class.

Characteristics of a Good Text-Book

The text-book helps the teacher to know what he has to teach; it helps the students to revise what has been taught to them in the classroom. Only a good text-book will help in this matter. The selection of a good text-book has to be done by the teacher. The teacher should keep the following points in mind while making such a selection:

(1) It presents the subject-matter strictly in accordance with the latest syllabus.

(2) It is written by experienced teachers.

(3) It is written according to the aims and objectives of teaching of Mathematics.

(4) It presents the subject-matter in a proper sequence. It may be so organised that it may be possible for the students to revise what they have learnt in the class. An effort be made to present the topic in a spiral form.

(5) It should contain well-graded problems for revision.

(6) The books be so written that they awaken intellectual curiosity of the students and also keeps their interest alive.

(7) The language of the book should be in accordance with the age group of the students.

(8) The printing and get up of the book should be attractive.

(9) It should suggested the teaching method, the possible aids for teaching the topic, correlation of the topic and the activities or practical work connected with the topic.

(10) It should contain well-illustrated material but not too many solved problems. The answers giving to problems should be correct.

(11) It must also contain objective type and short answer questions.

(12) Hints for difficult problems be provided.

(13) It should be moderately priced.

(14) It should give only up-to-date material.

Thus to evaluate a Mathematics text-book, the criterion may be useful content material, proper organisation of subject-matter, proper gradation of the exercises, material aid devices for motivation, simple language, good number of illustrations, good printing and an impressive get up. It should be moderately priced and free from mistakes and errors. It should not contain too many solved problems and should be up-to-date in its contents.

8.4 TASK OF WRITING TEXT-BOOKS

To write a text-book is not an easy task. Text-books must be planned in a scientific way and the subject-matter be presented in a psychological way. Text-book should not only present the subject-matter but should present it in a manner suitable for the students. The subject-matter be arranged to meet the requirements of the age and stage of the students. The various qualities of good text-books have already been discussed and these qualities must be found in good text-books.

8.5. TEXT-BOOKS OF CIVICS FOR VARIOUS STAGES OF EDUCATION

The various stages of education are : (1) Primary, (2) Junior High School, (3) Secondary, and (4) Higher.

In the present chapter, we are not concerned with the text-books of pre-primary and higher stages of education. We are primarily concerned with the text-books to be used in the Primary, Junior High School and Secondary classes. Text-books meant for these various stages of education should have certain qualities and requisites as laid down below :

(i) **Text-books of Civics for Primary Classes.** Here the students up to the age of 11 come to receive education. Such children are very fond of listing to stories. Curiosity is their basic instinct. Text-books that are intended for this stage of education, should have the following qualities in them :

(1) The subject-matter should be presented in form of a story.

(2) Books should be profusely illustrated. There should be a good deal of charts and pictures.

(3) They should be written in a simple language and lucid style. This would enable the students to understand the subject-matter easily and quickly.

(4) The text-book should be written with an eye on the psychological requirements of the children of this age.

(5) These books should not be very bulky.

(6) The subject-matter of the book should be based on the principle of selectivity. Such subject-matter should find a place in these text-books that shall be useful for developing certain requisite qualities in the children of this age group.

(7) The book should be perfectly in accordance with the syllabus and the curriculum laid down for this stage of education.

(8) The title cover should be very attractive so that it may catch the eyes of the students at the first glance.

(9) Books should be reasonably priced. These should be cost too much as to be beyond the reach of the common man.

(10) They should intend at inculcating social qualities in the students.

(11) The main aim of teaching Civics is to produce ideal citizens of the country. The seeds for ideal citizenship should be shown at this stage of education, with the help of these text-books.

Activity and creativity should be developed in the students with the help of these text-books. In other words, it means that the subject-matter should be so presented that there may be a good deal of scope for creative activities in the students.

(ii) **Text-books of Civics for the Students of Junior High School Classes.** At this stage of education students between the age group of 11 and 14 are found. These students are on the gateway of adolescence. They do not take interest in listening to stories only. They want to face the realities of life to some extent. Text-books of Civics, in tended for the students of this stage of education, should be written in more or less narrative style. They, in order to be useful, should have the following qualities :

(1) Text-books of Civics for this stage of education should be written with an eye on the mental and the physical age of the students. They should keep in view the interest, aptitudes and talents of the student.

(2) The subject-matter should be properly graded.

(3) At the end of each chapter there should be certain questions for recapitulation.

(4) The printing and the get up of the text-book should be flawless and attractive.

(5) There should be charts, pictures, illustrations, etc. These charts and illustrations should be attractive, precise and neatly drawn.

(6) The text-books should form to the aims and objectives of the teaching of Civics at this stage of education.

(7) They should also develop the qualities of ideal citizenship in the students.

(8) An attempt should also be made to develop the social qualities in the students.

(9) Civics is a subject which requires more of practical training than theoretical teaching. Text-books should aim at this objective. This training has to begin at the Junior High School stage of education.

(iii) **Text-books for Secondary Classes of Education.** This is the stage of adolescence. Students between 14-18 years of age come and receive education at this level. They are interested in taking a practical view of life. They want to solve problems by themselves. Their curiosity of listing to stories has come to an end. Certain other instincts and tendencies start developing by now. The text-books in order to be useful successful, should cater to these psychological needs. They should have the following characteristics as well :

(1) Firstly, they should be different from the text-books intended for the students of the Primary and the Junior High School classes. There is little scope for story telling and dialogues at this stage of education. There should be narration of facts. This narration should be of a realistic nature but interesting.

(2) The subject-matter of the text-books should be so organised that it may satisfy the mental faculties of thinking, reasoning, imagination etc.

(3) The subject-matter should be properly selected. It should be so selected as to meet the requirements of the psychological needs of this stage of education.

Problems of social, political and moral value should form the subject- matter of teaching at this stage of education. It is natural for text-books to present these problems in an interesting and effective manner.

(4) Students of this age and fond of solving the problems. Various problems concerning civic life should be so presented before the students, of course, through text-books, that they may take an active part in them and try to solve those problems.

(5) Text-books of Civics for the students of Higher Secondary classes should have a good number of graphs and charts in them. These graphs and charts are helpful in encouraging the students to take up serious study of Civics.

(6) There is scope for giving facts figures in the text-books meant for this stage of education. These facts and figures should be recent ones.

(7) The language and the style of the text-books of this stage of education has a specific importance. The style should be lucid, no doubt, but it should be well-polished. The language should be easy but it should be able to convey the thoughts properly and effectively. The subject-matter should be properly organised and categorised. The sequence of the sentence should not be

very complex. In short, an attempt should be made to present the subject-matter in an attractive and effective manner.

(8) The subject-matter of the text-books should be properly co-related. An attempt should be made to co-relate the subject-matter of Civics with that of History, Political Science and such other social science that have a direct bearing on the subject-matter of Civics.

(9) Since the subject-matter of Civics is more of a practical nature, an attempt should be made to employ Project Method, Problem Method. Activity Method, Excursion Method etc. in its teaching. An attempt should be made to reflect these methods in text-books as well.

(10) Subject-matter of Civics is of a changing nature. Every year we find some changes in the structure of the administration or the working of the civics life. The text-books should be kept up-to-date.

(11) The text-books for this stage of education should be reasonable priced.

(12) At the end of every chapter, there should be a set of questions. These questions should be psychologically planned and scientifically presented. They should help the recapitulation of the subject proves taught.

In short, the text-books should meet all the requirements of this stage of education. Text-books of Civics are not very up-to-date. Following extract from Secondary Education Commission Report proves this point further :

"We are greatly dissatisfied with the present standard of production of school books and consider it essential that it should be radically improved."

Revision Questions

1. Bring out the importance of text-books in teaching of civics.
2. What is the utility of text-books in teaching of civics ?
3. What are the characteristics of good text-book ?

Chapter 9

The Civics Teacher

9.1 INTRODUCTION

The success or failure of a civics course rests mainly with the teacher. He may be provided with all the possible facilities in terms of laboratory, apparatus and equipment, given an ideal syllabus and a sufficient time for teaching civics but unless he is enthusiastic about his work, knows the subject and really knows how to teach civics, he is not likely to achieve success. On the other hand a keen and well-informed teacher who loves his subject and believes in its value will succeed inspite of difficulties and handicaps.

In this regard the Kothari Commission Report (1966) says, "Of all the different factors which influence the quality of education and its contribution to national development, the quality, competence and character of teachers are undoubtedly the most significant."

Dr. S. Radha Krishan emphasises the role of teacher in the following words, "The teachers place in society is of vital importance. He acts as the pivot for transmission of intellectual traditions and technical skill from generation to generation, and helps to keep the lamp of civilisation burning. He not only guides the individual, but also, so to say, the destiny of nation. Teachers have therefore to realise their special responsibility to the society. On the other hand, it is incumbent on the society to pay due regard to the teaching profession and to ensure that the teacher is kept above want and given the status which will command respect from his student.

9.2 PLACE OF THE TEACHER

Independent India has by common consent adopted democracy as the best form of government. Democracy however needs a body of citizens who are ever prepared to shoulder the responsibilities that go with freedom. To have such citizens tomorrow, we must develop in our children and youth of today the knowledge, competence and sense of values that would make them effective members of the nation. In this respect civics can contribute the most. A great responsibility, therefore, devolves upon the teacher of civics. He must thoroughly prepare to meet the challenge.

Teacher is the real source of education. Truly speaking education is a tri-polar process and consists of *child (pupil), subject-matter,* and the *teacher,* child is the focal point (central part) around which the whole process revolves. The *teacher* tries to teach the *child* the *subject-matter.* While teaching the child, the teacher has to keep an eye on the psychological requirements of the child. It is the teacher who actually guides the destiny of the child. Teacher handles the subject-matter in such a way that the students are equipped for their future life. For any nation to progress we need a team of successful teachers. If a nation has only in competent teachers it is sure to go down.

In the words of Prof Bining, "Teacher is the pivot around which whole educational system moves."

The teacher is like a gardner who tends the tender plants of society and help them to blossom forth into full bloom and fragrance. The teacher of civics in this regards tries to fill the fragrance of ideal citizenship into the future flowers of civic life of the land.

9.3 ROLE OF POLITICAL SCIENCE AND CIVICS TEACHER IN THE LIFE OF THE SCHOOL

A political science and civics teacher is expected to play a very important role in the life of the school. Some of the roles expected of him are :

(i) Serving on school committees.

(ii) Working with parents.

(iii) Counselling students.

(iv) Filling out reports.

(v) Acting as a home room teacher or house master.

(vi) Serving on duty around the school.

(vii) Having contacts with school officials.

(viii) Issuing grades and reports.

(ix) Taking part in co-curricular activities.

(x) Working with clerical staff of the school.

(xi) Taking part in social affairs with teachers and students.

(xii) Taking part in community activities.

(xiii) Assisting student teachers.

(xiv) Participating in professional activities.

(xv) Performing miscellaneous duties in the total life of the school.

Duties of the Teacher of Civics

The main duties of the teacher of Civics is to inculcate in the students the values of ideal citizenship. In order to achieve this objective he has to undertake the following jobs :

(1) Teacher should act as a student. In other words, he has to study the interest, aptitudes and other mental faculties of the students and impart knowledge of Civics to them with an eye on all these mental faculties.

(2) He should keep himself up-to-date about the problems of civic life. He should know the most recent events of the civic life.

(3) No curriculum of Civics can be complete and up-to-date. Civics is an evergrowing subject. The teacher of Civics has to act as a Curriculum Construction Expert. He has to fit in the different developments of the civic life in the curriculum in such a way that the students may not feel that he is reading something that is not of interest and of value to him.

(4) The Civics Teacher is to act as a link between the School and the civics life at large. He has to establish co-relationship between the life and the school and the life of various other associations and social groups. The main aim of teaching of Civics is to establish and ideal civic life. It is the duty of the Civics Teacher to encourage the students to play their role in this direction.

9.4 QUALITIES AND CHARACTERISTICS OF A SUCCESSFUL CIVICS TEACHER

In order to achieve the above mentioned objectives and to discharge the tasks expected of a Civics Teacher, he should have the following qualities:

(1) Ideal citizen.

(2) Faith in the teaching of the subject and profession,

(3) Thorough knowledge of the subject,

(4) Impartiality and scientific outlook,

(5) Sympathy and creative imagination.

(6) Impressive and interesting personality,

(7) Faith in democracy,

(8) Love and affections for the students,

(9) Ideal social worker,

(10) Ideal leader, and

(11) Properly equipped.

1. Ideal Citizen. According to an old saying "Example is always better than a precept." The teacher of Civics has to prove this saying all the more by his actions. Civics has a practical aspect as well. It has to train young students to become ideal citizens. A teacher of Civics has to present the example of ideal citizen to be able to encourage the students to acquire the qualities of ideal citizenship.

2. Faith in the Teaching of the Subject and the Profession. The teacher of Civics should have faith in the profession as also the utility of teaching Civics of the students. Unless a person has faith in the job that he is entrusted, he will not be able to do full justice to it. This faith encourages a person to acquire more and discharge his duties in an ideal manner. The teacher of Civics should have this faith in him.

Unless the teacher is convinced of the utility of teaching Civics, he shall not be able to do justice to the subject.

3. Thorough knowledge of the subject. The teacher should have a thorough knowledge of the subject. If he has no command over the subject he shall not able to present the subject-matter before the students in an interesting manner. The teacher of Civics should know the correlationship of Civics with other social sciences. He should also be aware of the current events and the duties of a citizen. He should also know where the interest of the nation lies. Unless he has all these qualities in him he shall not be able to teach the students successfully.

4. Impartiality and scientific outlook. The teacher of Civics should be impartial. He should try to present the subject-matter in an objective manner. If he is not able to do that, he shall not be able to inculcate the spirit of true citizenship in the students. If the teacher colours the subject-matter with his personal views and likes and dislikes, he shall not be doing justice, either to the students or to the subject.

The presentation of the subject-matter should be systematic and proper. It can be possible only if the teacher has a scientific outlook.

5. Sympathy and creative imagination. The elements of sympathy enables a person to understand things properly. This quality also helps the teacher to know the viewpoints of the students. Creative imagination helps the teacher to present the subject-matter in a lively and interesting manner. Ross has remarked that the person from whom a gift of Sympathy is withheld should not become teacher.

6. Impressive and interesting personality. Personality of the teacher plays an important role in the classroom. If the teacher has an impressive and interesting personality he is able to impress the students well. It is quite possible that a teacher may have certain drawbacks in the personality but he can overcome them by certain other accomplishments.

7. Faith in democracy. Citizenship is very much needed for a democratic way of life. Unless the teacher has full faith in democracy and democracy way of life, it shall not be possible for him to teach Civics properly. For efficient functioning of democracy the citizens must know their rights and duties. They have to be conscious of their social obligations and needs. Only such teacher, who has full faith in democracy, can teach all these things to his students.

8. Love and affection for the students. The teacher of Civics should have a mastery of child psychology and educational psychology. Unless he has the knowledge of all these things as also the knowledge of the method of teaching and the principles and objectives of teaching, he cannot discharge his job successfully. The teacher who is endowed with all these qualities, shall have love and affection for his students. He should treat the students as if they were his own kith and kin and would treat them sympathetically. Such an atmosphere is congenial for teaching, specially for the teaching of Civics.

9. Ideal social worker. The teacher of Civics makes an effort to build the lives of his students. This life building can be possible only when he is intimate with the spirit of social service. Developing the students into ideal citizens in the greatest social service that can be done. The teaching of Civics has the practical aspect in this respect. This teacher of Civics should act as a social worker and inculcate in the students the spirit of social services and ideal citizenship.

10. Ideal leader. The teacher of Civics should have the qualities of an ideal leader. A teacher who has this quality is able to impress the students more. He is able to guide the students in the proper direction. Since teaching of Civics has the practical aspect as well, an ideal leader can lead his followers in the right direction.

11. Properly equipped. The teacher of Civics should be properly equipped. He should know the method of teaching as well as other requirements of a teacher. As already stated he should have the knowledge of child psychology as well as educational psychology. If he has these qualities he will be able to do real job. Prof. Hardikar has summed up these qualities in the following words :

> "A teacher of Civics must be, in short, himself a good and worthy citizen, like an American citizen in the days of Pericles. Only a citizen-teacher can induce 'civic consciousness' in his pupils."

Eight C's of an Effective Political Science and Civics Teacher

(i) Content mastery

(ii) Confidence

(iii) Caring for the pupils

(iv) Communication skill

(v) Creativity

(vi) Curiosity

(vii) Commitment

(viii) Catalytic power.

Nine Special Qualities of a Civics Teacher

(i) Art of development of human relations

(ii) Objectivity

(iii) Deep knowledge of the subject

(iv) Application of field study theory

(v) A well-informed teacher

(vi) Widely travelled person

(vii) A good communicator

(viii) Skilled in the use of technological aids

(ix) An interpreter of various experiences.

9.5 SELF-APPRAISAL BY A POLITICAL SCIENCE AND CIVICS TEACHER

A civics teacher may evaluate himself by taking into consideration the following points :

A. Attitude Towards the Subject

1. Does my attitude towards the teaching of civics stress facts to the neglect of ideas ?
2. Do I obtain most of my social knowledge from books ?
3. Do I observe events and trends in my community with a reasonable degree of insight and critical judgement ?
4. Do my assignments emphasise facts at the expense of interpretation of critical judgement ?
5. Do my tests give students an opportunity to exhibit that they have passed from memorisation to such procedure as comparison, contrast, selection, evaluation, deduction and judgement ?

6. Do I help my students to interpret successfully the meaning of factual material ?
7. Do I help students to use terms with precision ?
8. Do I try to restrain excessive use of emotion in the thought processes of students ?
9. Do I encourage the students to ask questions that show the development of capacities higher than that of memory alone ?
10. Do students show a capacity to apply in civics those procedures that are expected in science—collecting and cataloguing the facts and drawing conclusions from them ?
11. Are students becoming increasingly aware of the importance of relevancy in the discussion of a subject ?
12. Am I constantly relating civics to the lives and experiences of students ?
13. Am I assisting students to work out a satisfactory compromise between the rigorous of abstract thinking and the human need for satisfying emotional loyalties ?
14. Am I assisting students to adjust their thought processes and attitude to the changes in the social world about them ?
15. Do I arouse students' interests' in my subject and acquaint them with its cultural and vocational values ?
16. Do I set up a provocative environment for the reconstruction of experience, utilising many school and community resources ?
17. Do I use community resources to like the subject with life ?
18. Do I seek professional growth continuously by such procedures as study, travel, meeting professional conference, etc.?

B. Attitude of the Political Science and Civics Teacher Towards Students

1. Do I provide every student in my class, work so suited to his abilities and needs that he can succeed with reasonable effort ?
2. Do I treat my students with reasonable courteous considerations ?

3. Do I respect each individual's personality ?

4. Do I have faith in the realisation of the best potentialities of each individual ?

5. Do I keep my classroom atmosphere free from an intensely competitive atmosphere ?

6. Do I stimulate students to discover and evaluate their own ability, strengths and weaknesses and to meet difficulty or criticism in a constructive way ?

7. Do I try to understand my students rather than to judge them ?

8. Do I watch the trend of the developing interest and attitude of my students ?

9. Do I respected the right of every student to have confidential information about himself withheld except when its release is authorised in his or public interest ?

10. Do I avoid disparaging remarks about child which might undermine his confidence ?

C. Attitude of the Teacher Towards Democratic Principles

1. Am I an example of democratic values ?

2. Do I act as a democratic group leader ?

3. Do I organise democratic groups which widen the area of common concern and encourage social leader ?

4. Do I provide conditions by which social control will come out of the group situation ?

5. Do I arrange learning experiences which are based on the interests, capacities and needs of the children and which have continuity with life ?

6. Do I provide conditions out of which arise opportunities for co-operatively solving a wide variety of problems and evaluating outcomes ?

7. Do I share in formulating the purposes, policies and methods of the school ?

8. Do I try become integrated into the community through active participation in the social life of the group ?

9. Do I aid in the achievement of new cultural patterns which extend freedom ?

10. Do I discuss controversial issues from an objective point of view thereby keeping the class free from partisan opinion ?

D. Attitude of the Political Science and Civics Teachers Towards Parents and Colleagues, etc.

1. Do I provide parents with information that will serve the best interests of children ?

2. Am I discreet with information received from parents ?

3. Do I adhere to any reasonable pattern of behaviour accepted by the community for a professional person ?

4. Do I refrain from discussing confidential and official information with unauthorised person ?

5. Do I deal with other members of the profession in the same manner as I myself wish to be treated ?

6. Do I speak constructively of other teachers ?

7. Do I honestly report to responsible persons matters involving the welfare of the students,the school system and the profession ?

8. Do I accept no compensation from producers of instructional material when my recommendations effect the local purchase or use of such teaching aids ?

9. Do I recognise that everyone has some strength and weakness ?

10. Do I keep quite when I see fault in others ?

11. Do I pick appropriate time and opportunity to ask for help or advise from others ?

12. Do I expect everything to go my own way ?

Revision Questions

1. What are the various characteristics and qualities of an ideal civics teacher ? Discuss.
2. A teacher can 'foster the qualities of ideal citizenship'. Examine the statement and comment.
3. Describe the functions of civics teacher and throw light on his chief qualities.
4. What should be the attitude of a civics teacher ?
5. Write a short essay on qualities of a successful civics teacher.

Chapter 10

Evaluation in Civics

10.1 INTRODUCTION

Once a teacher has a clear of what she will teach and how she will teach it, she is concerned with knowing to what extent children learn from her lessons. This chapter will deal with specific procedures for evaluating the effectiveness of civics teaching-learning.

Evaluation is a continuous process which is an integral part of teaching. It is not merely a test at the end of a civics lesson or unit. Instead, evaluation goes on constantly during lessons and units and is clearly related to the teacher's goal and points of view on geography teaching.

Besides being a continuous experience, evaluation is cumulative. A cumulative civics record should be kept for all children. If such a record is available then his civics exposure can be quickly and easily seen.

The recent trends in learning and evaluation link them to behavioural objectives. According to behaviourist psychology learning is defined as a *charge in the behaviour of an individual that can be described in terms of observable and measurable performance.* The changes in behaviour are effected by providing experiences and through teaching.

The test efficiency of teaching, to judge the progress of students and to discover their achievements and evaluate the whole school system, we require some sort of measuring tools. These tools are *tests or examinations*. Tests are essential to grade and rank pupils, however if evaluation is used merely to indicate areas of civics to which children have been exposed or for classifying and categorizing students, a great value is lost. The same loss occurs if evaluation is interpreted only as arriving at numerical or alphabetical ratings for report cards. In this way much of the positive use of evaluation as a means of teaching and learning could be destroyed.

Effective instructional planning and evaluation of students performance have always stressed upon statement of instructional objectives so that they are of great help to the student. According to Muller, an instructionally usable objective must state the intended outcome in terms of the terminal behaviour of students. Terminal behaviour here stands for the behaviour of students after the classroom instructions and evaluation can be made if the learning outcomes are carefully specific. By coupling continuous evaluation with immediate application of what has been learned, the teacher can provide for—

(i) The stimulation of students who learn rapidly to greater growth towards goals by application of advanced works.

(ii) The identification of specific weaknesses and difficulties in functional understanding (concepts, principles, generalisations) and the needed reteaching of varied activities, skills or problem solving abilities, and

(iii) The clarification, modification or complete alternation of the goals as needed for the unit.

Evaluation teaching and learning are the three corners of the education system. *Evaluation* is connected with finding out how far students have learned as a consequence of teaching. There are two kinds of evaluation depending upon whether the comparison of student is made with some absolute performance standard or with other students of a given group. These are known as *criterion referenced evaluation* and *norm reference evaluation.*

10.2 MEANING OF EVALUATION

Evaluation is the inclusive concept. It indicates all kinds of means to ascertain the quality value and effectiveness of desired outcomes. It is a compound of objective evidence and subjective observations. It is the total and lineal estimate.... It is a valuable and indispensable guide to the modification of policies and to further action. In other words, we can say that evaluation is the approval of pupils progress, in attaining the educational goals set by the school, class and himself. The chief purpose of evaluation is to guide and further the students learning. Evaluation is thus a positive rather than a negative process.

10.3 IMPORTANCE OF EVALUATION OR EXAMINATION

Examination system is the test of the knowledge acquired. In the present set-up of education it is this very system which helps us to ascertain the efficiency of a student in a particular subject. Examination are of two types:

(a) Written or theoretical, and

(b) Oral.

Written tests are 'essay type tests'. Probably it is the type of test which makes the students feel unhappy and nervous about their examination days. Various scholars have given various epithets to this type of examination. Some of these are given below :

(1) A bane of educational system

(2) A blood sucker

(3) A necessary evil

(4) An obstacle to learning

(5) An enemy of true education etc., etc.

Examinations are conducted to measure the achievement. This measure of achievement is known as *evaluation* or *examination*. Unless we are able to have proper assessment and evaluation of the achievement. The achievement becomes meaningless. This process helps a person to improve his achievement. This is what shall be more clear from the following lines :

> "Evaluation signifies a wider, more comprehensive and continuous process of assessing student progress. It is integrated with the whole task of education and its purpose is to improve instruction and not merely to measure its achievement. In its highest sense evaluation brings out the factors that are inherent in student growth such as proper attitude and understanding."

There is some distinction between examination and evaluation. Examination is slightly less comprehensive while evaluation is more. In fact, evaluation is a new technical term. It connotes a comprehensive concept of measurement. J. W. Wrightstone has rightly remarked :

"Evaluation is a relatively new technical term introduced to designate a more comprehensive concept of measurement that is applied in conventional test and examinations..... The emphasis in measurement is upon single aspects of subject-matter achievement or specific skills and abilities....The emphasis in evaluation is upon board personality changes and major objectives of an educational programme. This includes not only the subject-matter achievement but also attitudes, interests, ideals, ways of thinking, work habits and personal and social abilities."

In others words, it means that it is the evaluation examination that helps not only the improvement of the achievement but also improvement of different traits of personality.

10.4 PURPOSE OF EVALUATION

Evaluation fulfills the following purposes :

(i) It assesses the extent of learning by students and gives them the feed-back about their performance.

(ii) It gives feed-back to the teacher about the learning gaps of the students. It also provides the teacher a feed back about the quality of his classroom instructions .

(iii) It provides the student an opportunity to show his worth.

(iv) It serves as a screening tool for selecting students for special purposes.

(v) To assess the success of educational system or the methods of teaching.

(vi) To provide educational, vocational guidance and counselling.

(vii) To examine the utility of the techniques and aids of teaching.

(viii) To find the aptitudes and inclinations of the students.

(ix) To encourage the process of learning.

(x) To bring about reforms in teaching and curriculum.

Our evaluation has another goal besides assisting the teacher in assessing and modifying her teaching procedures. This goal *self-evaluation* is not solely for the students. As teacher and students actively engage in all levels of a study such as initial planning, organisation and carrying out activities they can be guided in developing ability to evaluate themselves. Knowing the general and specific goals can aid the pupil in checking himself all along the way. This makes the learner an active participant in class room activities. It also places some of the responsibility on him for learning and assessing what and how much he has learned. Self-guided evaluation stimulates healthy and realistic achievement goals. A logical first step in self-evaluations is setting up of realistic goals These goals for civics teaching in elementary schools are :

(i) *Functional understandings* such as concepts, principles, generalizations, and the facts needed.

(ii) *Problem solving* skills such as defining problems, proposing hypotheses and techniques necessary for the solution of the problems, observational techniques, discussion and interpretations skills.

(iii) *Scientific attitudes, interests and appreciation* such as open mindedness and humanity.

The easiest are to evaluate is functional understanding because a rich variety of test are well-known and are widely used in elementary schools. Before we proceed to actual discussion of these tests let us consider the criterion of a good examination and pre-requisites of a physical test.

10.5 CRITERIA OF A GOOD EXAMINATION

Though a variety of tests are available to test the functional understanding of the child but for true assessment of such aspects of growth as the elements of reflective things, scientific attitudes, resourcefulness, creativeness or such other objectives or interests we require more precise and accurate instruments of evaluation. According to most of the psychologists and educationalists the following are essential criteria of satisfactory evaluation.

1. *Validity.* Any good test should measure what it claims to measure.

2. *Reliability.* A good test is one that is reliable i.e., it gives same rating to a candidate even if he is examined by different examiners and even at different times.

3. *Objectivity.* A test can be considered objective if the scoring of the

test is not affected in any way by the examiner's personal judgment. Thus the opinion, bias or judgment of the examiner can have no influence on the results of on objective test.

4. *Comprehensiveness.* By comprehensiveness of a test we mean that it covers the whole or nearly the whole course content and the questions are uniformly distributed to cover the course content.
5. *Practicability.* A test is called practicable if it can be easily administered and is acceptable to average examiners. While preparing such a test, the time and cost of administration must be taken into consideration. The test should be usable and should serve a definite need in the situation in which it is used.
6. *Interpretability.* A test can be considered as interpretable if its score can be used and interpreted in terms of a common base having natural or accepted meaning.
7. *Easy to Administer.* A good test should be easy to administer so definite provision be made for collection and preparation of test material. It should give simple, clear and precise instructions.

Pre-requisites of a Good Test

There are certain pre-requisites for preparing a good test. These are as under.

Aspects		*Description*
Aims	—	Acquisition of knowledge of various political concepts and skills.
	—	Development of scientific attitude and interest.
	—	Development of laboratory skills.
	—	Highlighting the application of civics/politics in every day life.
	—	Development of skills of information processing, observation, enquiry and design.
	—	Acquisition of problem solving abilities.

Aspects	*Description*
Objectives	
(a) *Knowledge :*	Recall and recognition of factual information such as (i) Definitions of various terms. (ii) Statement of laws, principles, rules, conventions etc. (iii) Description of construction and working of devices and instruments. (iv) Description of events, processes and phenomenon. (v) Recognising the parts of devices, instruments, appliances and apparatus. (vi) Identifying known physical phenomenon, events and occurrences.
(b) *Comprehension :*	Understanding facts, laws etc (i) Comparing and contrasting various phenomenon. (ii) Locating error, limitations and defects. (iii) Illustrating scientific phenomenon. (iv) Reasoning events on the basis of certain principles and laws.
(c) Applications :	Using knowledge in new situations (i) Solving numerical problems. (ii) Making use of various laws in various situations and events. (iii) Relating various variables.
(d) Skills :	Using psycho-motor skills (i) Laying out an experimental set-up. (ii) Drawing diagrams, graphs, histograms, flow charts etc. (iii) Reading various measuring instruments.

(e) *Analysis :* Breaking up information into parts of reach conclusions

(i) Interpretation of observations.

(ii) Drawing inferences from observations.

(iii) Generalising conclusions.

(f) *Synthesis :* Combining parts of information to grasp a concept

(i) Designing an experiment

(ii) Improvising an experiment, apparatus or device.

(iii) Improving the accuracy of an instrument.

10.6 TYPES OF TESTS OR EXAMINATIONS

Generally, the test are of three types :

(1) Traditional or essay type examinations.

(2) New type test or examination.

(3) Dissertation type test.

Traditional Types of Test or Traditional Type of Examination

It consists of only form of questions and that is essay type questions.

New Type of Examination or Test

These tests are known as objective test. They consist of the following types of tests :

(1) Recall type of test.

(2) Alternate response type of test.

(3) Multiple choice type of test.

(4) Matching type of test.

(5) The completion type of test.

(6) Classification type of test.

Defects of Traditional Type of tests or Examinations

At present new type of test are taking the place of traditional or essay type of tests. This trend is gaining importance because traditional type of examinations suffer from following defect:

(a) Defects from the Point of View of Students

(i) The essay type tests are less objective and so they lack validity. This type of test can reveal child's cramming capacity only.

(ii) These tests lack reliability. A student is compelled to have a selective reading. He depends more on guess papers and so there is an element of chance.

(iii) It keeps the students busy and full of nervous tension. The study does not spread over the whole year and is limited to a short period just before the examinations. Thus a habit of irregular study is developed in the student.

(b) Defects of Essay Type Examination from the Point of View of the Teacher

(i) The teacher covers only a limited and important portion of course because his aim is to see that maximum number of his students pass the examination.

(ii) The teaching programme of the teacher is wholly examination oriented and the basic principle of teaching his students are given least consideration.

(iii) The teacher is compelled to encourage his students to cramming which is not a psychological method of teaching.

(iv) Since a teacher is judge by the results of his students so every thing becomes subservient to the examinations.

(v) To show good results sometimes the teacher devotes a good deal of his time to indulge in guess work which affects his teaching.

(c) Defects from the Point of View Achievement

(i) Essay type tests are not comprehensive and some students may get good marks only because the questions have been set from the portion prepared by them.

(ii) These tests are not objective and the score of a student depends on various factors such as Examination's mood and whims etc.

(iii) This type of tests are not useful from the point of view of improvement. They fail to throw light on the defects of teaching-learning process or the defects of the cur¬iculum.

From the above it can be concluded that essay type examination is not a correct method of evaluation in Mathematics. The improvement in system of evaluation is possible if following suggestions are given due consideration.

(a) Improvement in Essay Type Examination

In essay type examination an improvement is possible if we set shorter questions spread over the whole course. The language of question should be clear and precise, clear cut directions be given for scoring.

(b) The Use of Objective Tests

In addition to essay type tests, some objective type tests may also be used for evaluation. The objective type tests can be of the following types:

(a) True-false type.

(b) Completion type.

(c) Multiple choice type.

(d) Matching type.

(e) Short answer type.

(c) Use of Oral Tests

In such tests oral questions are given and students are required to give answers after oral calculations. Such tests require quick recall and thinking. These test help in assessing the ability of the students to apply the knowledge of facts in different situations.

(d) Assessment of Regular Work

For such an assessment a record of child's development should be kept. Such a record may be kept for his home-work, practical work etc., and this should be take into consideration while assessing a student.

Thus, we find that no single device is enough and a judicious blend of various evaluation tools is the best approach.

10.7 OBJECTIVE TESTS

At present objective tests are used for evaluation. The objective tests consist of completion type test, matching type tests. True/false type tests etc. Such objective tests have following merits :

(i) The objective tests have little or no scope of subjectivity. The score does not depend on Examiner's mood or whims.

(ii) These tests are more reliable. The score does not depend on expression, speed, style etc.

(iii) These are comprehensive. This requires from the students, thorough study of the syllabus.

(iv) There is no chance element in this type of tests.

(v) These are easy to administer and easy to score.

(vi) These are economical in respect of time.

However, they also suffer from certain drawbacks. Some of these are as under :

(i) The objective type tests fail to test the organising ability of the students.

(ii) These tests fail to develop thinking and reasoning powers of the students which is one of the main aims of teaching Mathematics.

(iii) These tests put more emphasis on factual knowledge and very little importance is given to processes, methods or originality of thought.

(iv) These tests encourage guess work.

(v) These tests are not diagnostic. Because they do not show the defects in the teaching-learning process.

(vi) These tests may pose some administrative difficulties as there may be indiscipline in the students. They may use unfair means, wishper answers or make some gestures.

(vii) It needs a lot of time and labour for preparing such a test.

Different Types of Objective Tests

We have already seen the various types of objective tests. Let-us now describe each of them in some detail.

1. Recognition Type of Test

Through this method, an attempt is made to assess the power of recognition of the student. In this method the student has to find out the correct answer out of several answers given. There are several sub-forms of this type of test. They are given below :

(a) Alternate response type or true/false test.

(b) Multiple choice test.

(c) Matching type test.

(d) Classification type tests.

(a) Alternate response type or true-false test. In this type of test, the answer is limited to the possibilities of true and false. Two alternatives are given and the examinee has to choose one. Sometimes the signs of '✓' and '✗' are also required to be used.

Example of the response type or true/false test:

Note: Given below are certain statements. But the letter 'T' against the statements that are true and 'F' against the statements that are false:

(1) Pakistan invaded India in 1965.

(2) Dr. V.V. Giri is the Prime Minister of India.

(3) The Prime Minister of India is elected by the people directly.

(4) Mr. C. B. Gupta is the Chief Minister of Uttar Pradesh.

(b) Multiple choice type test. In this type of test, several answers are given to a particular question. The student is asked to find out the correct answer.

Example

Note: Given below are several answers to a particular question. Put the sign '✓' against the correct answer.

(1) India secured freedom on January 26, 1948/August 15, 1947/ January 26, 1950.

(2) Mrs. Vijai Laxmi Pandit/Mrs. Sucheta Kripalani/ Mrs. Indira Gandhi/Mrs. Tarkeshwari Sinha/Mr. P.V. Narasimha Rao is the Prime Minister of India.

(c) Matching test. In this type of test, the examinee is provided with two lists. In these lists, the subjects are not given in a serially ordered manner. The student expected to serialize them and put them against each other. For example:

1. Dr. Sankar Dayal Sharma	Prime Minister of India
2. P.V. Narasimha Rao	President of India
3. Y. B. Chavan	Finance Minister of India
4. Dr. Man Mohan	Foreign Minister of India.

(d) Classification type of test. In this type of test, the student is given a group of certain words. Out of these words, generally one word is irrelevant. The student is asked to underline that word. For example

Note: Underline the word that is irrelevant.

Uttar Pradesh/ Punjab/ Haryana/ Maharashtra/ Bangalore/ Kashmir/ Orissa.

2. Recall Type of Test

In this type of test, the power of recall of the student is judged. He is asked to answer the questions that test his recall power. Following are the various types of recall type of test:

(1) Simple Recall type of test; and

(2) Completion test.

(1) Simple Recall type of test. In this type of test, the students are expected to answer the question on the basis of their memory. Given below is an example of this test:

(a) When did India get freedom ?

(b) Who was the first President of India ?

(c) When Did Sri Lal Bahadur Shastri die ?

(2) Completion test. In this type of test, the examinees are given incomplete sentences. They are supposed to complete the sentences filling in proper words in the blank places. Given below is an example—

(i) The Prime Minister of India is the leader of the —— party in Parliament.

(ii) The member of Rajya Sabha receive a monthly allowance of Rs.——.

Requirements of the New Type of Test

New type of tests have to be carefully constructed. The following precautions be taken otherwise, these tests are likely to lose the utility :

(1) Careful planning and construction.

(2) These tests should be carefully planned and constructed only then they shall serve their purpose. For this the following things are needed :

(a) *Determination of the Purpose.* The basic purpose of the test must be decided first.

(b) *Selection of the Test in Accordance with the Purpose.* After the purpose has been decided, the test has to be found out which would suit the purpose.

(c) *Objective Questions.* The questions that are constructed should be objective.

(d) *Ability of the Students to be kept in Mind.* The individual differences and the mental ability of the students should be kept in mind, otherwise the purpose shall not be served.

(e) *Scoring Key to be Prepared.* The scoring key, that provides answers to the questions, must also be prepared. Unless it is done, the purpose shall not be served. Without this, it shall be difficult to award marks.

(f) *Standardization.* These tests need standardization. Then only it is possible to do away with the element of subjectivity.

(g) *Intelligent Planning.* It is not possible for all the teachers to plan these tests. These tests have to be planned and constructed by intelligent teachers as they require intelligent planning.

Other Types of Tests. In addition to the tests given above, the following types of test are also used :

(a) *Intelligence Test.* The basic objective of these tests is to ascertain the mental capacity or the psychological capacity of the students. These tests require such questions that would give an idea about the mental age of the students.

(b) *Recognition Test.* These tests have the element of the traditional examination as also the new system of examination. In these tests, a figure is drawn or a particular question is given and the students have to recognise it. It may be very easily applied to Geometry.

(c) *Logical Selection Test.* In this test, several names of a particular object are given. The correct and the exact name is to be sorted by the students. This is also a new type of test.

Importance of Blue-print in Constructing Achievement Test

The blue-print here means the plan that the teacher has in evaluating the performance of the pupils.

The blue-print concerns itself to the knowledge acquired by means of study, remembering, thinking, solving problems and formulating hypothesis. It is here that the formulation of instructional objectives and their respective behavioural changes can be clearly identified.

In a blue-print the objectives are listed out horizontally. They are knowledge, understanding, application and skill. Again horizontally forms of test items are indicated. They are essay questions, short answer questions and objective questions.

Vertically we find the content divided into sub-units. The question paper should cover all the sub-units and all the objectives. The score for each type of question viz, essay, short answer and objective type should be fixed.

Dissertation Type of Tests

In this type of examination the examinee has to carry out research work as a prescribed topic. He has also to present dissertation that contains the results of the work done by him. The plan of this work is submitted in writing. In fact, it is an enlarged form of the essay type test.

Revision Questions

1. Giving the meaning and purpose of evaluation, throw light on the importance of evaluation in civics.

2. Discuss the importance of evaluation in civics.
3. What are the defects of existing system of examinations ? Give your suggestions for its improvement.
4. How does a new type attainment test differ from traditional test ? Illustrate your answer with two types framed on civics syllabus prescribed for any stage of education.

Chapter 11

Planning Civics Lessons

11.1 INTRODUCTION

Though a syllabus is prescribed for each class yet the teacher is at liberty to draw up his own teaching syllabus. Planning is essential not only in teaching but in all spheres of human activity. R.L. Stevenson said, "To every teacher I would say, always plan out your lesson before hand but do not be a slave to it." Bagley has put it thus, "However able and experienced the teacher, he could never do without his preliminary preparation."

To be effective in his job everybody plans before hand e.g. A surgeons plans well in advance before putting his patient on the operation table, the house-wife plans the details of daily meals etc. So must a teacher plan and prepare his work.

11.2 LESSON PLANNING AND ITS IMPORTANCE

A proper planning of lesson is the key to an effective teaching. The teacher must know in advance the subject-matter and mode of its delivery in the class-room. Thus gives the teacher an idea of how to develop the key concepts and how to correlate them to real life situations and how to conclude the lesson. Lesson planning is also essential because effective learning takes place only if the subject-matter is presented in an integrated and correlated manner and is related to the pupil's environment. Though lesson planning requires a hard work but it is rewarding too.

L.B. Stands conceives the lesson plan as 'plan of action' implemented by the teacher in the classroom. According to G.H. Green, "The teacher who has planned his lesson widely related to his topic and to his classroom without any anxiety, ready to embark with confidence upon a job he understands and prepared to carry it to a work manable conclusion. He has foreseen the difficulties that are likely to arise, and prepared himself to deal with them. He knows the aims that his lesson is intended to fulfill, and he has marshalled his own resources for the purpose. And because he is free of anxiety, he will be able to Coolly to estimate the value of his work as the lesson proceeds, equally aware of failure and success and prepared to learn from both."

Nelson L. Bossing explains the meaning of lesson plan in these word, "Lesson Plan is the title given to a statement of the achievements to be realised and the specific means by which these are to be attained as a result of the activities engaged in day-by-day under the guidance of the teacher." This definition tends to focus the teacher's attention upon :

1. Outcomes or result in terms of the Pupil's achievement.
2. Definite processes and procedures with a recognition of activity as the basis of learning.
3. The pupil in the foreground and the teacher in the background as guide and director only of the learning activity.

A lesson plan indicates the aim to be realised by teaching a lesson, the methods to be employed and the activities to be undertaken in the class so that it is kept engaged for the realisation of the aim. A lesson plan is actually a plan of action. It includes :

(i) The working philosophy of the teacher.

(ii) His information and understanding of his pupils.

(iii) His comprehension of the objectives of education.

(iv) His knowledge of material to be taught.

(v) His ability to use effective methods of education.

Aims of the Lesson Plan

The lesson plan is expected to show the following things :

(i) The knowledge that the students have acquired.

(ii) The direction towards which the students have to be carried, and the new subject-material that they have to the taught.

(iii) In the beginning we have the general aims and objects of the teaching and in particular, aims and objects of teaching of that subject.

(iv) There is also a statement of experience of the teacher.

(v) It aims at presenting a systematic knowledge of the subject of the students.

Functions of Lesson Plan

Important functions of lesson plan are as follows:

(1) It delimits the field of work of the teacher as also of the students and provides a definite objective for each day's work.

(2) Since the goal is fixed so teacher gets an impetus to achieve his goal.

(3) It prevents the teacher from going off the track.

(4) It helps the teacher to organise and systematise the learning process.

(5) It helps in avoiding needless repetition.

(6) It helps the teacher to overcome the feeling or nervousness and insecurity. It gives him confidence to face the class.

(7) It provides opportunity to the teacher to think out new ways and means of making the lesson interesting and to introduce thought provoking questions.

(8) In ensures a definite assignment for class and availability of adequate materials for the lesson.

Importance of Herbart in the Field of Lesson Plan

Herbart was the man who introduced this system of Lesson Plan. He was an idealist and believed in imparting education to the students for building up their character. In order to achieve this objective, he gave an important place to the teacher in the educational set-up. He gave a general method to be utilised by the teachers for imparting knowledge to the students in the class-room. With the help of this method he could achieve the objective of building of the character of the students.

Four steps of Herbart

Herbart has laid down the following four steps in his method for teaching. He has said that the Lesson Plan or method of teaching should have the following qualities :

(1) Clearness or clarity,

(2) Association,

(3) System, and

(4) Method.

Additions of Zillar. Zillar was a disciple of Herbart. He has made an attempt to improve the method of the teaching of Herbart. He has divided the step of clearness into two sub-divisions; namely,(a) Introduction, and (b) Presentation.

Generally, this whole plan is known as five steps of Herbart. This plan of education is said to be very useful in the teaching of Science and Mathematics, but with certain modifications, it can also be utilised for the teaching of other subjects as well. In the following pages we have tried to apply this method in drawing of the lesson plans of Civics.

Features of a Lesson Plan

Some important features of a good lesson plan are as under :

(i) *Objectives :* All the cognitive objectives that are intended to be fulfilled should be listed in the lesson plan.

(ii) *Content :* The subject-matter that is intended to covered should be limited to prescribed time. The matter must be interesting and it should be related to pupil's previous knowledge. It should also be related to daily life situations.

(iii) *Method(s) :* The most appropriate method be chosen by the teacher. The method chosen should be suitable to the subject matter to be taught. Suitable teaching aids must also be identified by the teacher. Teacher may also use supplementary aids to make his lesson more effective.

(iv) *Evaluation :* Teacher must evaluate his lesson to find the extent to which he has achieved the aim of his lesson. Evaluation can be done even by recapitulation of subject-matter through suitable questions.

11.3 TYPES OF PLANNING

(a) Planning of the work of the year in a definite manner and in unit.

(b) Planning of each unit.

(c) Daily lesson planning.

(d) Planning shared with the pupils.

11.4 UNIT PLANNING

A unit is related learning segment made up of a few lessons alongwith an outline of its actual execution in the classroom. Thus a unit will consist of both the subject-matter and methodology of its delivery to students.

Hoover defines units as, "The teaching unit is a group of related concepts from which a given set of instructional and educational experiences is desired. Unit normally range for three to six weeks long."

In view of Preston, a unit is a large chunk or a block of related subject-matter as can be over viewed by the learner.

After having divided the prescribed syllabus into a number of teaching units the teachers will decide the time that could be allotted to each unit. After that he can break up each unit is a number of lessons and each lesson should be complete in itself. After this the teacher will enter in his diary the scheme of work under the headings.

Some of the advantages of unit planning are as under :

(i) It provided a basic course structure around which specific class activities can be organised.

(ii) In enables the teacher to integrate the basic course concepts and those of related areas into various teaching experiences.

(iii) It provides an opportunity to the teacher to keep a balance between various dimensions of the prescribed course.

Unit No..................

Date	*Course content*	*Demonstration*	*Equipment material*	*Student's activities*	*Remarks/ References*

(iv) It enables the teacher to break away from traditional text-book teaching.

If the prescribed course has to be covered in a number of years then it is unitwise to distribute the course in units spread over a number of years.

11.5 STEPS IN LESSON PLANNING (HERBARTIAN STEPS)

Formal steps in lesson planning are :

1. Introduction (or preparation)
2. Presentation
3. Association (or comparison)
4. Generalisation
5. Application
6. Recapitulation.

1. Introduction

It pertains to preparing and motivation children to the lesson content by linking it to the previous knowledge of the student, by arousing curiosity of the children and by making an appeal to their senses. This prepares the child's mind to receive new knowledge. This step though so important must be brief. It may involve testing of previous knowledge of the child. Sometimes the curiosity of pupil can be aroused by some experiment, chart, model, story or even by some useful discussion.

2. Presentation

It involves the stating of the object of lesson and exposure of students to new information. The actual lesson begins and both teacher and students participate. Teacher should make use of different teaching aids to make his lesson effective. Teacher should draw as much as is possible from the students making use of judicious questions. In science lesson it is desirable that a heuristic atmosphere prevails in the class.

3. Association

It is always desirable that new ideas or knowledge be associated to the daily life situations by citing suitable examples and by drawing comparisons with the related concepts. This step is all the more important when we are establishing principles or generalising definitions.

4. Generalisation

In science lessons generally the learning material leads to certain generalisations leading to establishment of certain formulates, principle or laws. An effort be made that the students draw the conclusions themselves. Teacher should guide the students only if their generalisation is either incomplete or irrelevant.

5. Application

In this step of lesson plan the knowledge gained is applied to certain situations. This step is in conformity with the general desire of the students to make use of generalisation in order to see for themselves if the generalisations are valid in certain situations or not ? No lesson of science may be considered complete if such rules, principles, formula etc., are not applied to life situations.

6. Recapitulation

In this step of his lesson plan the teacher tries to ascertain whether his students have understood and grasped the subject-matter or not. This is used for assessing the effectiveness of the lesson by asking students questions on the contents of the lesson. Recapitulation can also be done by giving a short objective type test to the class or even by asking the students to label some unlabelled sketch.

One most important point to remember is that the six steps given above for lesson planning are formal Herbartian steps and teacher should not try to follow these very rigidly. These are only guide lines and in many a lessons it is not possible to follow all these steps.

There is another way of lesson planning which is gaining currency these days. It is known as *Glover Plan.* This plan has four steps as follows:

1. **Questioning.** Teacher must introduce and develop his lesson through related and sequential questions. Start the lesson by asking questions about previous knowledge of the students. The questions should then lead to new knowledge under consideration.

Lesson can also be introduced with the help of some teaching aid like a picture, chart or model etc., the introduction can also be made by describing a situation or by telling a short story.

However, teacher should hear in mind that the introduction is brief and interesting.

2. **Discussion.** For discussion the class be divided into smaller groups and in such groups students be encouraged to express their ideas and opinions freely. This helps the students in removal of their difficulties.

3. **Investigation.** The students are encouraged to do a project or investigation on the lesson topic either individually or in small groups by processing information or be laboratory work.

4. **Expression.** It concerns the strategy in which the student's and the teacher's communication of ideas through observation and listening (passive expression) or through doing (active expression) or through fine and performing arts (artistic expression) or by arranging learning situations (organisational expression).

In developing a lesson a teacher must keep in mind the following psychological principles.

(i) *Principle of Selection and Division.* The teacher should wisely select and divide the learning material into smaller segments. It is also for the teacher to decide about the quantum of subject matter to be covered by him and that which has to illicited from the students.

(ii) *Principle of Successive Clarity.* It is for the teacher to see that the different learning segments of lesson are well-structured, sequenced and connected. Teacher must ensure, at each segment, that students have grasped the subject-matter given to them.

(iii) *Principle of Integration.* Teacher should conclude his lesson only after combining various learning segments to produce some generalisation.

Design for Writing a Lesson Plan

Lecture-Cum-Demonstration Method

The style given below is generally followed for writing a lesson plan.

Class: Date:

Subject : Duration

Topic : of period:

Instructional Material ____________________

General Objectives ____________________

Specific Objectives ____________________

Previous Knowledge ____________________

____

Questions

1. ____________________?
2. ____________________?
3. ____________________?

Introduction ____________________

Questions ____________________

1. ____________________?
2. ____________________?

Announcement of Aim ____________________

____

Presentation

Matter	*Method*	*B.B. Summary*

____

Generalisations ____________________

____

Applications ______________________

____

Recapitulation ______________________

Questions ______________________

1. ______________________?
2. ______________________?
3. ______________________?

Home Task ______________________

11.6 MODEL LESSON PLAN

Class : VI

Subject: Civics

Topic: Functions of District Board

Date :

Period: 4th period

Duration: 40 minutes

General Aims:

Specific Aim :

To teach the students about functions of District Board

Teaching Aids:

Previous Knowledge

Q. Have you got any arrangement for sanitation of your village ?

Ans. Yes.

Q. Who looks after these arrangements ?

Ans. Employees of the District Board.

Q. What are the Functions of District Boards ?

Not getting a proper reply to this question the teacher will announce to the students the aim of his lesson.

Announcement of Aim and Introduction

To introduce the lesson the teacher will announce to the students, today we shall study about the functions of the District Board Presentation.

Presentation

Matter	*Method*	*B.B. Summary*
Sanitation and Cleanliness of village is necessary, because the roads are 'kucha' and in rainy season the water causes a lot of mud. There is no arrangement of drainage, the dirty water flows around and spoils the passage. There is dirt and mud all around. Zila Parishad looks around all these arrangements.	Why is the cleanliness of your village necessary ? The conditions of village roads and town roads will be compared by showing pictures of both type of roads (teaching aid)	(i) Roads are 'kucha'. (ii) In rainy season the passages are spoiled due to flow of dirty water. (iii) Zila Parishad looks after these arrangements i.e. construction of roads, arrange for drainage etc.
Zila Parishad is also responsible for organising fairs and exhibitions and deputing its officials to inocculate people when an epidemic breaks out. Primary schools are also run by Zila Parishad.	What are the other functions of Zila Parishads ? Who organise fairs? Who runs primary schools ? Who arranges for inocculation when epidemic breaks out ?	(i) To organise fairs. (ii) To run primary schools. (iii) To inocculate people when an epidemic breaks out.

Recapitulation

(i) Name the body that looks after the sanitation of your village.

(ii) Give various functions of Zila Parishad.

Home-Task

Write in your note-book briefly the functions of Zila Parishad.

Revision Questions

1. Describe briefly the things that are required for drawing a lesson plan.
2. What is the importance of lesson planning in the teaching of civics ? Give an outline of a lesson plan in civics.

Chapter 12

Values of Civics Teaching and Teaching of Civics at Various Stages in India

12.1 INTRODUCTION

Teaching of civics is of great importance and value to the society. Values are nothing but the end or the objectives that are achieved by doing a thing. Teaching of civics is carried out keeping the following values in mind :

1. Character-formation
2. Development of the qualities needed for an ideal society.
3. Development of the outlook of the citizens.
4. Hygienic outlook.
5. Proper use of science.
6. Knowledge of political problems and development of capacity to solve them, and
7. Social outlook.

12.2 VALUES OF TEACHING CIVICS

1. Character-Formation. Mudaliar Commission on Secondary Education made a thorough study of the structure of the secondary education in India. In its report, the Commission has tried to give due place to various subjects in the curriculum. While talking about the importance and the value of teaching of Civics, it has been said that it leads to character formation. The teaching of civics brings about the development of the qualities of co-operation, kindness, sympathy, shouldering of responsibility, etc. It is these qualities that have great value in the social set up.

2. Development of the qualities needed for an ideal society. Teaching of civics brings about the development of those qualities which are essential for an ideal social set up. Civics helps children to understand the complex society. The spirit of co-existence, and spirit of 'Live and Let Live' can be acquired only through the teaching of Civics. This quality is very much needed for an ideal society.

3. Development of the outlook of the citizens. Our country is faced with various social and political problems such as untouchability illiteracy, low status or women etc. These problems can be solved only if the citizens develop a scientific outlook with respect to all these things. Teaching of civics is quite useful in the development of such an outlook. It also helps the citizens in the solution of these problems.

12.3 PRESENTATION OF SUBJECT MATTER OF CIVICS AT DIFFERENT STAGES OF EDUCATION

Various Stages of Education

(i) Primary Stage : **Age** 6-11 years, **Classes** 1-5

(ii) Junior High School Stage : **Age** 11-14 years, **Classes** 6-8

(iii) Secondary Stage : **Age** 14-18 years, **Classes** 9-12

(iv) University Stage of Education

Our interest at present is only in the first three stages of education.

Principles of the Presentation of Subject-Matter

Following are the basic principles that the teacher has to bear in mind while presenting the subject-matter before the students of the various stages of education :

(1) The matter that is presented should be factual and intelligible.

(2) The teacher should make an effort to present the subject-matter with an eye on the age, mental growth, needs, interests and aptitudes of the students.

(3) Only theoretical presentation of the subject-matter is not sufficient for a successful teacher. He should also lay stress on the practical importance of the knowledge.

(4) In the earlier stage children are prone to imitation. The teacher should present himself before the students in such a way that

they may do such things that are good for education and the work in the class. This means that the conduct of the teacher should be an ideal for the students to copy.

(5) Co-ordination is the essence of teaching of civics. The teacher should try to correlate the subject-matter of civics with life. This shall help the students to use the subject-matter in their practical life.

(6) The teacher should try to proceed from single to complex and from concrete to abstract. This will be the scientific method of teaching.

Presentation of the Subject-material

On the basis of the cardinal principles stated above, we shall now try to study the presentation of the subject-material at various stages of education.

PRESENTATION OF THE SUBJECT-MATERIAL AT THE PRIMARY STAGE OF EDUCATION

As already stated, at this stage children of 6 to 11 years of age group are taught. They are fresh from the family life. At attempt should be made to conduct their life in such a way that they may develop the social qualities. The development of the social qualities shall be helpful for their future life.

Children of this stage are very fond of listening to stories. They have a lot of curiosity in them. In other words, curiosity is the basic instinct at this stage of life. The teacher should base his presentation of the subject-material on the basis of this instinct. He should utilise the instinct of the curiosity of the students and their fondness for listening to stories. In other words, the subject-matter should be presented in the form of stories. The teaching should be through the story method.

How to Select a Story ?

(1) The story should be so selected that it may develop the activity of the students.

(2) The story should be in accordance with the interests and mental age of the children.

(3) The story may be historical as well as imaginary.

(4) Every story should present one or the other ideal of civics.

(5) Other precaution (a) *Use of text-books.* The teacher should not use the text-book very much at this stage of education. Books that are utilised should be profusely illustrated.

(b) The nature of the story should be simple. The teacher should try to narrate the story in a natural manner and at a speed that the students can follow. Short sentences should be used.

(c) The students should be given practical education to the maximum possible extent.

(d) Through stories, civic qualities should be developed in the students. An attempt should be made to develop those qualities arid habits in the students that may be helpful in their practical life.

(e) Through drill method or exercise, the training of the discipline may be given.

Use of the Black-board. Black-board can be used at this stage. It should be used for explaining the pronunciation of the names to the students. The teacher should write out very legibly on the black-board. Too much use of black-board shall not be useful.

The writing on the black-board should be very good. If the teacher writes a good hand it shall encourage the students to imitate it and also improve their hand-writing.

The students should also be given the training of expressing their ideas.

Excursion, trips and tours shall also be helpful. Through these methods the training may be imparted.

Dialogues. If an attempt is made to teach the students certain principles of civics through dialogues, it shall be an interesting method. In the lower classes the dialogues should be very short but interesting. In Class V, the dialogues may be of one to two minutes of duration. But this process should not be carried out for more than 10 to 15 minutes.

Use of charts, maps, pictures, models, etc. These are in fact the teaching aids that make the lesson interesting. The teacher should present these things in the classroom while teaching Civics. He may also encourage the students to copy these things.

As far as possible only essential things should be taught to the students at this stage education.

At this stage of education the students of the age group of 11 to 14 years are taught. They are slightly grown up children. They are not the children who are fond of listening to stories. They do not live in the world of imagination. They are actually heading towards maturity and adolescence. At this stage children start using their power of thinking and reasoning. It means that they are no more fond of listening to stories. Only fairly tales cannot be interesting for them.

The teacher should now change their course of action and method of teaching. The teacher should now keep an eye on the developed brain and the real vocabulary and the knowledge of the students. The subject-matter should be presented to them in a practical manner.

Story Method. Story method can be used at this stage as well. But this method should not be of the type that is used at the primary stage of education. The teacher should use the story method as and when required. But now the story should be of slightly developed nature. They should develop in the students certain civic qualities.

Teaching Methods. So far as methods of teaching are concerned, observation, narration, question-answer, project and dramatic methods may be employed.

The teacher should also take the students out on tours and excursions and make them see the working and the building of the Municipalities, Corporations, Panchayats, Zila Parishads etc.

Text-Books. At this stage it is useful to employ text-books. But these text-books should not be read out in the class. They should be used by the students at home for revising the lessons that they have learnt in the classroom.

Supplementary books may also be used by the students.

The students should also be encouraged to take to practical work. These practical works should be directed towards ideals of teaching of civics.

Black-board. As compared to the primary stage of education black-board should be used more at this stage. The teacher should draw sketches, maps, graphs, etc., on the black-board and explain the topics, with the help of these things, to the students. The students should also be encouraged to come and write on the black-board.

Models, charts, maps etc. All these things should be used at this stage of education. They strengthen the experience of the children. The students should be encouraged to draw these things themselves.

Radio and films may also be used at this stage of education.

Home-Task. Home-task should begin at this stage of education. The teacher should ask the students to do some home-task. The teacher should himself examine the home-task with interest. If the teacher is interested in the home-tasks the students shall also be interested in it.

Most of the teaching should be oral but the written work must start of this stage.

PRESENTATION OF THE SUBJECT-MATERIAL AT THE SECONDARY STAGE OF EDUCATION

Mental and actual age of the students. At this stage of education, teacher has to deal with adolescents. In these boys the power or reasoning, thinking, arriving at decisions etc., have found development. Their physical development has also taken place. The teacher has now to take into consideration the interests, aptitudes and the talents of the students. He has to organise his teaching with an eye on these things.

The physical development of the students also start taking place in new way. At this stage of education, Self-regarding Sentiment, finds a development. The teacher has to bear in mind these things as well. He should not try to insult the students. On the other hand, the students should be encouraged to do things in a way that they get appreciation at the hands of the members of the society.

Moral development by this time has taken place. Their vocabulary also grows rich by this time. The teacher should utilise all these things for the benefit of teaching civics.

This is called the 'Age of Organisation'. In other words, it means that the various talents and faculties of the children start organising themselves. The teacher should arrange the teaching with on eye on this aspect of the personality as well.

Use of Text-Books. Text-books should be compulsorily used at this stage. The students should be encouraged to repeat and revise their class-room lessons with the help of the text-books, at home. They should be encouraged to prepare notes with the help of the text-books.

The teacher should ask the students to write out answers of certain questions. These questions should be such as to encourage and awaken the various mental powers of the students.

The students should be trained in the art of self-study. Interest in self-study should be created by the teacher. They should be asked to go to Library and select out good books of History. The teacher should help them in this task.

Discussions. At this stage students should be encouraged to take part in discussions and debates. In the classroom such discussions may be organised. These discussions and debates will improve the power of thinking, reasoning, etc., of the students.

The students should be encouraged to undertake tasks of responsibility in the school. They should also be encouraged to form voluntary bodies and take part in students' Government. These organisations should be so directed that they take to healthy activities. Such activities will generate and strengthen the civic qualities of the students. They shall also prepare the students for their future life.

Use of Black-Board. Black board should be used but sparingly. The teacher should put down substances and other short notes. The students should be encouraged to develop that substance in the form of essays etc.

Models, charts, maps etc. These things should be used to make the lessons interesting. But these things should be of a developed nature.

Tape recorders, radios, films, newspapers, magazines etc., may also be used to add to the knowledge of the civics. With the help of these things the teacher can make his subject-material quite interesting.

At this stage of life, students are very fond of roaming about. An excursion to place of civic importance will add to their interest and knowledge of civics.

Students should also be acquainted with the current events of social, political, religion and moral importance. They should be encouraged to take active interest in gathering information about all these aspects of life.

An attempt should be made to make the teaching practical as far it is possible.

12.4 INDIAN SCHOOLS AND THE TEACHING OF CIVICS

The importance of Civics as a subject lies in its utility to the society. Its importance has been recognised in India, but we have to face certain problems in its teaching. Our educational system is as such that a student of the subject gets only the theoretical knowledge of a subject. However, Civics is a subject which has its practical utility. It is said that even after the thirty five-years of independence, we have not been able to give a practical shape to the theoretical knowledge acquired by us in the field of different social science and same is the case with civics also.

In the teaching of civics in the Indian schools we have to face the dirersified problems. Some of them are discussed here :

1. Aims of Teaching of Civics not clear. In Indian Schools, Civics is taught in such a way that the student is unable to know the real aim of the subject that he is studying. There are different aims of teaching of civics such as development of character, development of feeling or patriotism, development of mental power, consciousness about rights but the real aim of its teaching is to build 'man a man.' Ideal citizenship is the main aim of civics. It is the subject that teaches us to live and let others live. However, this aim is somewhat neglected in the teaching of civics in Indian schools.

2. Defective Curriculum. Some writers are of the opinions that the curriculum of the Civics is defective in Indian schools. In fact, the teaching of civics in Indian school starts at Junior High School classes. At this stages of study too much emphasis is lays on the theoretical knowledge. The practical value of the civics is more or less totally neglected. In High School and Intermediate classes too the case is almost is the same. In fact, the curriculum of Civics is as such that a student has to study the same topic from Junior High School stage upto Degree stage. The diversification of curriculum is totally neglected.

3. Inadequate aids. Teaching of civics can be imparted in an appealing manner only if the material aids are used properly. However, in our Indian Schools, the material aids are used in most of schools. We find only text-books and black-board for the teaching of civics. What to talk of audio-visual aids like radio, film, script, taperecorders, slides, projector and television even the visual aids such as model, lecture chart are not there. How can the teaching of the civics be effective when there are no proper material aids.

4. Defective teaching methods. In our Schools, the teaching of civics is imparted only through text-book method and lecture method, other methods of teaching like observation method, project method, unit method and laboratory method are almost neglected. In the teaching of civics all these methods lave their own importance but to lack of facilities and certain other things, we are unable to teach civics through all these methods.

5. Lack of proper arrangements. Civics is almost neglected subject in our schools. There are no proper arrangements for its teaching upto Junior High School. It is taught alongwith History and Geography. The result is that teacher gives more emphasise on Geography and History rather than civics. There are no properly decorated classrooms for the teaching of civics. The library facilities are also inadequate.

6. Death of good Civics Teachers. In a democratic country like India, the teacher of civics has an added value and importance because he trains the students for ideal citizenship and of democratic way of life. However, there is a great dearth of good civics teachers in our schools. Some as the teacher has no faith in the teaching of the subject. If the teacher himself is not an ideal citizen then how can he be expected to train the students. If the teacher himself is not democrat how can he be expected to train the students for the democratic way of life.

7. Defective system of Examination. In India the systems of examinations and valuation very defective. Much emphasise is being given or cramming. In almost all the schools, the system of essay type is prevalent. The objective type of test are rarely found. Generally, it is said that the written type of test or the essay type of examination is the correct method for assisting the achievement of the students. This statement is not wholly correct. Civics involves a lot of practical knowledge. It is, therefore, necessary to apply some sort of practical examination also to judge the attainment of the students. The students should be given an opportunity to take part in collective activities, organise work, parliaments, courts, assemblies and councils etc. They should also be given an opportunity to learn the art of proper exercise of their franchise. They should also be given responsible positions in the field of games and other activities. This provides them with an opportunity for acquiring the traits of leadership.

In the end, we may say that in our India schools, the teaching of civics is not properly imparted. All our efforts should be made to improve its teaching.

Revision Questions

1. What are the values of teaching of civics ? Discuss.
2. Discuss briefly the method of presentation of the subject-matter of civics at various stages of education.
3. What principles would you bear in mind in the presentation of the subject-matter of civics at various stages ? Discuss.
4. What are the problems of teaching civics in India schools ?

Chapter 13

Political Science, Civics Room and Museum

13.1 INTRODUCTION

For every subject a separate room in essential. For teaching literary subjects ordinary rooms may serve the purpose but for teaching of subjects like civics/political science a separate room is essential. Because of financial difficulties it is not possible for every school to have a separate civics room but it is desirable to have it and equip it with suitable material (equipment). In the absence of a civics room it would be difficult to collect all the material, needed for civics teaching, at a place and it is practically impossible to take these things from one place to another. Moreover in the absence of a separate room teacher will not get congenial atmosphere which is quite essential for effective teaching. It has been observed by M.P. Mofatt, "Classroom furnishings and their arrangements have direct bearing upon the quality of results obtained. Satisfactory outcomes can be expected from any classroom situation only when adequate facilities are provided. It should be furnished to provide a suitable environment for acquiring and practicing social studies skills."

A provision of a special room for political science and civics is desirable because of the following considerations :

(i) Providing 'home of their own' to teachers for developing enthusiasm for the subject and faith in themselves and students.

(ii) Creating and maintaining an effective teaching-learning environment.

(iii) Providing a quick and ready functional environment by making available work-room for the students.

(iv) Introducing variety in teaching methods and facilitating the use of teaching aids readily and conveniently.

(v) Saving energy and time in carrying round equipment like charts, maps, models, pictures and projectors etc.

13.2 EQUIPMENT OF THE POLITICAL SCIENCE AND CIVICS ROOM

It should be provided with the following equipments :

(1) Audio-visual material including film strip, epidiascope, projector, magic lantern, tape recorder etc.

(2) Bulletin Boards

(3) Charts and graphs

(4) Globes

(5) Maps and Atlases

(6) Flags

(7) Models

(8) Some meteorological instruments such as barometer, rain gaue etc.

(9) Rocks and minerals.

(10) Stamps.

(11) Survey instruments such as compass, chain, arrows, divider, scale etc.

(12) Slide album containing slides showing architecture, dancing, music, painting etc.

(13) Time charts and graphs

(14) Text-books

(15) Reference books

(16) Unit booklets dealing with different topics.

(17) Literary material

(18) Periodicals and magazines.

(19) Newspapers.

(20) Pamphlets published by various agencies including central and state governments and also agencies such as UNO, UNESCO etc.

13.3 POLITICAL SCIENCE AND CIVICS MUSEUM

Museum is quite expensive and cannot be provided for every school. However, if we keep a miniature museum it is possible to gain more by spending less. In a museum students came in direct contact with the nature and with the things taught in a class. Only those things which are essential for students be kept in the museum.

The Secondary Education Commission, on the role of school museums observed, "Museums play a great part in the education of school children as they bring home to them much more vividly than any prosaic lectures, the discoveries of the past and the various developments that have taken place in many fields of science and technology." Again the Commission observes, "We believe it is necessary from the educational point of view to establish such museums in important centres at least wherein both ancient and modern collections will be exhibited and in some cases even demonstrations given of the actual process of development of various scientific discoveries. Nothing can impress students in the formative age so much as the actual visualising of these experiments in a graphic manner."

These museum are made up of materials used in classroom teaching which, in many cases, are collected classified and exhibited by students, with or without the help of a teacher. The museum activities may be an extracurricular function of the class or the school or they may be incorporated into a scientific-experimental method of teaching. The objectives of this type of museum are :

(a) to form within the school or the classroom an embryonic community dedicated to the usual occupations reflected in the school life of adults;

(b) to permit visual instructional and experimentation with actual museum specimens;

(c) to stimulate enthusiasm for study and research among both teachers and students;

(d) to stimulate interest, co-operation and participation in the cultural activities and scientific research conducted by the large museums ;

(e) to instruct students in proper scientific methods of laboratory research and museum conservation and exhibition techniques;

(f) to from, in the absence of larger museums in the community, a nucleus from which the classroom museum cam grow beyond the limits of the school to serve ultimately the community and the region as a whole.

New exhibit programmes, interpretation, visual communication. What then are some of the ways in which museums as cultural and educational centres of the community can communicate successfully with their transitory visitors of heterogeneous composition ? Based on various audience-testing experiments the following media can be used to heighten the effectiveness of visual communication.

(a) *Dramatic labels.* Experiments suggest that large letters placed at the focal point of the case or exhibit area will successfully headline the exhibit and catch the visitor's attention.

(b) *Dramatic lighting.* Light is a means of visual communication as well as an attention getter. Coloured lights that change, fade or highlight an exhibit can be used with great dramatic effect. Light can also be used to tell a story and to convey a sense of passing time. Light is particularly important in art museums.

(c) *Dramatic utilisation.* Again experiments suggest that museum visitors should be given a chance to feel exhibits as well as to see them. Of course, much depends on the nature and expendability of the object involved but certain types of material—objects of wood, stone and metal and special "touch me" samples of animal skins and fabrics—can be used with great success to satisfy the visitor's urge to touch while permitting a minimum of danger.

(d) *Dramatic sound effects.* Sound, like light, can be used to heighten the dramatic effects of visual communication. For example, an Amazon rain forest exhibition can be made vastly more effective by adding the sound of tropical rain, the croaking of frogs, the chattering of monkeys, and the beat of drums. An exhibit of medieval art can be made more meaningful if it is accompanied by music of the same period.

Revision Questions

1. Make out a case for providing a separate civics-room in schools.
2. Make a list of equipment for a civics-room.
3. Discuss the role of museum in teaching of civics and political science.

Chapter 14

Miscellaneous

14.1 YOUTH PARLIAMENTS IN SCHOOLS

Objective of Youth Parliaments

The Department of Parliamentary Affairs of the Government of India has been implementing a scheme entitled 'Youth Parliament Competition Scheme for Recognised Educational Institutions in the Union Territory of Delhi'. The objective of the scheme is to strengthen the roots of democracy, inculcate healthy habits of discipline, tolerance of views of others and to enable the student community to know something about the working of the Parliament.

Guidelines for the Organisation of Youth Parliament

1. Seating arrangements inside the chamber of youth parliament. The working of Youth Parliament should broadly follow the pattern of the working of the Lok Sabha. It would facilitate the task of the teacher-in-charge of this activity, if he/she and the students, selected to participate in the youth parliament competition could first acquaint themselves with the practical working of the real Parliament of the country by witnessing the actual proceedings and make themselves conversant with the arrangements made for the members in the chamber of the Lok Sabha.

The lay-out of the chamber of their Youth Parliament should resemble (as far as possible) the lay-out of the chamber of Lok Sabha. The dias and chair of the presiding officer should be on the straight base of the semi-circle. The seating arrangement for members should be in the shape of horse-shoe as it is in the Lok Sabha. The chamber of Lok Sabha is a semi-circular hall with the speaker sitting in a canopied chair, placed conspicuously at the centre of the diameter connecting the two ends of the semi-circle. There is a dividing space in front of the speaker's rostrum. On the left of the rostrum are the seats for the opposition and on the right are the seats for the governments benches. Slightly raised above the chamber of the Youth Parliament for visitors are seat the 'press', the 'diplomats' and the 'distinguished visitors', etc.

2. Agenda. Generally the following items be included in the agenda for a sitting of Youth Parliament :

1. Oath of affirmation.
2. Obituary reference.
3. Questions.
4. Adjournment motion.
5. Questions involving a breach of privilege.
6. Papers to be laid on the table.
7. Call attention notice.
8. Legislative business.
9. Motions.

3. Start of the Session. Like the practice prevailing in Lok Sabha, the session of Youth Parliament starts with the arrival of the speaker, which is announced by the marshal of the house. The marshal, before announcing the arrival of the speaker, ascertains that there is a quorum in the house which should be at least 10 per cent of total membership of the house. Thereafter, the speaker presumes that there is a quorum at all times unless his attention is invited to lack of quorum. In either case bell is rung and the business of the house proceeds only when there is quorum in the house.

As soon as the speaker arrives in the chambers, marshal announces his arrival with the words "Honourable Members, the Honourable Speaker" and after this the entire house stands up. The speaker before taking his eat first bows to his left, then to his right and then in front of him. He then takes his seat. The members also respectfully bow to the chair before their seats.

4. Oath of affirmation by members. The speaker takes up the business of the house in the order in which it is printed in the list of business. The first item in the agenda is "oath or affirmation by the new members." Before taking the seat in the house every member is required to or subscribe an oath or affirmation in the following forms :

"I....having been elected (or nominated) a member of the House do swear in the name of God/solemnly affirm that I will bear true faith and allegiance to the Constitution of India as by law established, that I will uphold the sovereignty and integrity of India and that I will faithfully discharge the duty upon which I am about to enter."

The members may make oath or affirmation in Hindi or English or in any of the language specified in the 8th Schedule of the Constitution. Before taking the oath the member should bring with him the certificate of election granted to him by the Chief Election Commissioner. Members elected at by-election at the time of making and subscribing oath or affirmation are introduced to the house by the Minister of Parliamentary Affairs.

5. Questions. The first part of sitting each day in the Youth Parliament should be developed to oral questions, commonly known as starred questions. In the Indian Parliament it is the most popular hour for the Members of Parliament and also for the public. From the point of view of a minister it is the most searching test of his grasp on the items of business allocated to him, his ability to lead as well as his ready with when answering supplementaries. The question has been defined as an instrument whereby a member can elicit, describe and get information in any aspect of public administration. During the youth parliament competitions the judges give credit for the quality of questions asked and the quality of replies given by the ministers.

The teacher-in-charge of Youth Parliaments generally experience difficulties. The subject-matter of questions can be the day-to-day problems faced by the common citizens. For instance, it is a common experience to witness long queues before D.M.S.milk booths in Delhi. There is often a complaint against the inadequate supply of poor quality of milk supplied at their booths. This can form the subject-matter of a searching question about the performance of the Ministry of Food and Agriculture and also about the unsatisfactory performance of the D.M.S

6. Short notice questions. Where any question relates to a matter of urgent public importance it may be asked for oral answer by a member with notice shorter than the minimum time of 5 days (as far as the minister is concerned) in the Lok Sabha. If the speaker accepts the urgency, he can admit it at shorter notice after ascertaining the willingness of the Minister to answer it. When it is admitted and placed on the agenda it is called immediately after the question hour.

7. Adjournment motion. Adjournment motion seeks to raise discussion on some sudden or emergent matter of public importance that has arisen in the country or abroad, demanding the immediate attention of the government and the house. If the motion is in order, and if a least 1/10th of the members present of the Youth Parliament stand up in favour of leave being granted, the motion is admitted. If less than this number rise in their seats, the speaker informs the member concerned that he does not have the leave of the house to move the adjournment motion.

8. Calling attention motions. A member may with the prior permission of the speaker call the attention of a minister to a matter of urgent public importance and request him to make a statement thereon.

9. No mention of existing political parties. The participants should scrupulously avoid the mention of the existing political parties and the political personalities in the country. They should give imaginary or fictitious names to their parties and personalities. They should not give any impression that they have any learnings or bias for any political party or philosophy.

10. Respect to the chair. The participants should show utmost respect to the Chair. They should strictly abide by the decisions of the Chair and should have faith in his impartiality and judgement.

Every member while coming to the house for its sitting should bow to the chair and similarly while leaving the chamber should bow to the Chair.

Members should not sit with their backs to the chair. When a member wants to speak he should rise in his place to attract the attention of the Chair. No member should speak unless he or she has "caught" the eye of the speaker and has been permitted by the Chair by name or by a sing to speak.

Every member should resume his seat as the speaker rises to speak or class out "order, order" and also when any other member is in possession of the floor.

No member should rise or leave the house when the speaker is addressing the house. The speaker is always to be heard in silence.

Two members should not keep standing at the same time. Members should not distribute within the precincts of the house or inside the legislature questionnaire or pamphlets not connected with the business of the house.

11. No discussion on foreign matters. There should be no discussion on sensitive policy matters affecting the relations of our country with foreign friendly governments or which will prove embarrassing for the country and its present day government.

Terms Used in the Parliament

1. Adjournment motion
2. Adult suffrage
3. Amendment
4. Bell
5. Bell-division
6. Bell-quorum
7. Bill
8. Bill-government
9. Bill-money
10. Bill-private member
11. Call attention
12. Chairman
13. Constitution
14. Casting vote
15. Cut motion
16. Council of ministers
17. Constituency
18. Consideration of bills
19. Demand for grants
20. Demand for grants voting
21. Debate
22. Executive
23. Electorate
24. Government
25. Governor
26. Governor's address
27. President's address
28. Hour
29. Hour-question
30. Hour-zero
31. Introduction of bills
32. Judiciary
33. List of business
34. Leader of the ruling party
35. Leader of the opposition
36. Legislative assembly
37. Legislative council
38. Marshal
39. Minister
40. Motion of no confidence
41. Motion of leave
42. Motion of thanks
43. Parliament
44. Party

45. Party-ruling
46. Party-opposition
47. Promulgate
48. Point of order
49. Questions
50. Ruling
51. Subjudice
52. Supplementary grant
53. Supplementary questions
54. States
55. Speaker
56. Speaker-deputy
57. Summons
58. Unparliamentary word
59. Union Government
60. Upper house
61. Vote
62. Whip
63. Whip-government
64. Whip-opposition

Unparliamentary Expressions

Arrogant
Buffoon
Blackguard
Bloody
Bluff
Deceive
Disgraceful
Dishonest
False
Foolish
Fraud
Hoodwink
Humbug
Hypocrisy
Idiot
Impertinent
Indecent
Liar
Mean
Brute
Cheat
Coward
Criminal
Damn
Puppet
Ridiculous
Rouge
Rowdy
Scandalous
Shut up
Silly
Stooge
Stupid
Thief
Traitor
Ungentlemanly
Unscrupulous
Vindictive

14.2 ORGANISING UNITED NATIONS PUPIL'S SOCIETY IN SCHOOLS

Introduction

The United Nations started with lofty ideals. It gave expression to the urges and aspirations of the millions of people suffering from the devastations of world war. The UN movement for peace and progress on earth is to made the peoples' movement. If UN is reduced to a bureaucratic organisation completely alienated from the people, then it would be great tragedy for the humanity. The young generation that is going to take up the responsibility of enduring peace and progress of the world is to be educated on the principles, ideals, working and problems of the United Nations. This will help their emotional identification with the UN. This is the surest approach to the world-wide movement for peace and progress. Organising UN Pupil's Society in school is a step forward in that movement. Among the various activities of the society would be to organise projects.

ILLUSTRATIVE PROJECT

Objectives of the Project

1. This project will help students to know and analyse the causes—historical, geographical, economic, political, racial and psychological—of wars and the nature of damage and destruction caused by war. This will enable them to share ideas and feelings with regard to war.

2. This will enable them to study in detail the situations during the war, and recognise the forces, the environment and the persons responsible for war—how these forces and persons work overtly and covertly—and their motives.

3. The students will get an opportunity to assess the nature of destruction and the consequences—the extent of the loss of life and property—the weapons of annihilation—and how this destruction affects their lives and society.

4. The project will help the students to understand the problems, struggle, anxieties and aspirations of the people of other

countries.

5. Students will be encouraged to estimate the gains of long peace—the massive development and progress of man due to undisturbed peace.

6. The students will be enlightened that wars are caused by the misdeeds of a handful of organised war-mongers and the majority looks for peace, mutual understanding and mutual co-operation. There are organisations like the United Nations trying to establish peace, and prevent tension. The students will try to evaluate the contributions by the UN for peace and progress of the world.

7. This project will involve the students in carrying out programmes and activities in line with the ideals of the UN.

8. Students will be motivated to create strong public opinion against war and the forces that encourage war, and enlighten the common man on the causes and consequences of war, and the gains of peace and mutual understanding.

9. Efforts will be made to bring about behavioural change in students. They will develop hatred for war. They are likely to act as the harbingers of peace. They are expected to develop a broad outlook and wide vision on the tensions, sufferings and aspirations of other people, develop the skill in persuading others to avert the path of hatred and tension, and understand the utility of peace and co-existence of nations.

Plan of Activities

Students will draw up the plan of activities which will be implemented in four stages :

Stage 1. Analysis of the problems of peace by, (a) study of the background and history of war and the international conflicts of the present day world; (b) collecting pictures, posters, life sketches of statesmen, statements, paper cuttings, reflecting on world tension; (c) contacting representatives of embassies of various countries to know their point of views; (d) visiting spots where past battles took place or visiting war museums to collect informations on the devastations due to war.

Stage 2. Contracting local agencies or organisations of the UN to know the efforts for peace and progress made by the UN— its various other humanitarian activities.

Stage 3. Exchanging information and views with teachers and classmates, creating public opinion in favour of UN efforts for peace and progress through exhibitions depicting the devastation of war and gains of peace, through persuasions and education of the common people in defence and mutual understanding.

Stage 4. Starting a student movement for world peace by sending help, gift and note of sympathies to the children who are the victims of war and destruction, and by appealing to the politicians through the embassies to stop war, and restore peace on earth.

Activities. The activities of the association will be (1) study of literature on UNO; (2) survey and visits; (3) debate and discussion; (4) interview with leaders and embassy people; (5) exhibition and display of facts and figures of war; (6) mobilising public opinion in favour of peace; (7) co-operation and relief to the war victims.

